GRAPHIC THINKING FOR ARCHITECTS AND DESIGNERS

GRAPHIC THINKING FOR ARCHITECTS AND DESIGNERS

Paul Laseau

VNR VAN NOSTRAND REINHOLD COMPANY

New York

Library of Congress Catalog Card Number: 79-20493
ISBN: 0-442-26247-1
ISBN: 0-442-25698-1 pbk.

Manufactured in the United States of America

Published by Van Nostrand Reinhold Company Inc.
115 Fifth Avenue
New York, New York 10003

Van Nostrand Reinhold Company Limited
Molly Millars Lane
Wokingham, Berkshire RG11 2PY, England

Van Nostrand Reinhold
480 La Trobe Street
Melbourne, Victoria 3000, Australia

Macmillan of Canada
Division of Canada Publishing Corporation
164 Commander Boulevard
Agincourt, Ontario M1S 3C7, Canada

15 14 13 12 11 10 9 8 7

Library of Congress Cataloging in Publication Data

Laseau, Paul, 1937–
  Graphic thinking for architects and designers.

  Bibliography: p.
  Includes index.
  1. Architectural drawings.   2. Communication in architecture.   3. Architecture–Sketch-books.
4. Graphic arts.   I. Title.
NA2705.L38   720'.28   79-20493
ISBN: 0-442-26247-7
ISBN: 0-442-25698-1 pbk.

Foreword

Paul Laseau proposes two related ideas; the first is that of "Graphic Thinking," the second is graphic thinking as a device for communication between designer and designed for. The following brief remarks are addressed to the relationship between the two ideas.

Historically, building design was not so indifferent to human well-being, that "communication with the people" became an issue, until the act of drawing was divided into two specialized activities. The first was design drawing in which the designer expressed his or her ideas. The second was drafting used to instruct the builder.

Design drawing began and remains a means of generating ideas, for tapping initial concepts to be sorted out and developed or simply as an enjoyable activity. Drafting is an eight hour task performed daily, filling sheets of paper with precise lines dictated by others.

Long ago when the work of individual craftsmen became larger and more complex, when a cathedral rather than a chair was to be designed, dimensions had to be established so that the work of a single craftsman could be coordinated with the work of many. Drawing was introduced as a creative device for planning work.

Craftsmen have always used drawings to help them visualize their ideas as they made adjustments in the continuous process of fitting parts together. Drawing under these conditions is inseparable from the work itself. Some historians say that the working drawings for the great churches of the twelfth and thirteenth century were drawn on boards which were later nailed into the construction.

But drawing also has other purposes. Productivity is increased by the division of labor. Artifacts requiring several weeks of work by a single skilled craftsman are divided into smaller standardized work tasks. Production is increased as skill is eliminated. The craftsman's expression of material, design sense and sketches are banished from the workplace. All facets of the work are predetermined by drawings and specifications.

Design decisions are given to a new class of workmen who do not work with the material but instead direct the actions of others and communicate their decisions to those who work through drawings made by draftsmen. Designing, as a separate task, has come into being. The professional designer, the professional draftsman, and the assembly line occur simultaneously as related phenomenon.

This all occurred some time ago but the momentum of the change from craftsmanship to draftsmanship, brought about by the peculiar form of industrialization we have chosen to adopt, persists. It now extends to the division of labor in the designer's office. The building of great buildings is no longer the creation of master craftsmen led by a master builder but of architectural offices organized along the lines of industrial production. The task of the architect has been divided and subdivided into an assembly line of designer, construction manager, interior designer, decorator, structural, electrical mechanical engineers, and draftsmen. Design decisions once made by the designer on the drawing board are now made by the programmer on computer printouts.

There are those of us who believe that industrialization could have been achieved without destroying the craftsman's skill, love, and respect for material and the joy of building. We find it even less desirable for the joy of creativity and graphic thinking that accompanies that activity should leave the designer's office for the memory bank of a computer.

The built world and artifacts around us are evidence of the almost fatal error of basing design on the mindless work of the assembly line. To develop programming and operational research based on mindless design would be to continue a disastrous historic continuum.

Graphic thinking is of course necessary to help rejuvenate a moribund design system. But communication, "with the people" is not enough. Creativity itself must be shared, and shared with everyone from dowel knocker to "lieber Meister". The need for graphic thinking is great but it is greater on the work benches of the assembly lines at River Rouge than on the desk of the chief designers of Skidmore, Owings and Merrill.

FORREST WILSON

Preface

In the fall of 1976, while participating in a discussion group on design communication at the University of Wisconsin-Milwaukee, I had the occassion to mention my book *Graphic Problem Solving.* Essentially that book was an attempt at convincing architects to apply their freehand concept-gathering skills to non-traditional problems dealing more with the processes than the products of architecture. During the discussion, Fuller Moore stated that the graphic skills I had assumed part of architectural training, were being neglected in the schools and that a more basic book on drawing in support of thinking was needed. Soon after, I had the chance to talk to several architects about the sketches they use to develop designs in contrast to the finished drawings they use in the presentation. Most creative architects had developed impressive freehand sketching skills and felt comfortable sketching while thinking. Some architects drew observations or design ideas in small sketchbooks they carried with them at all times. Both the architects and the educators I interviewed expressed concern over the apparent lack of freehand graphic skills in people now entering the profession.

As I began to collect materials for this book, I wondered about the relevance of sketching in architecture. Could sketching be better

applied to designing as practiced today? The answer to this question depends on an examination of the present challenges to architectural design:

1. To be more responsive to needs, a problem-solving process.
2. To be more scientific, more reliable or predictable.

The response to these challeneges was suggested by Heinz Von Foerster: "... the language of architecture is connotative language because its intent is to initiate interpretation. The creative architectural space begets creativity, new insights, new choices. It is a catalyst for cognition. This suggests an ethical imperative that applies not only to architects but also to anyone who acts on that imperative. Act always so as to: increase, enlarge, enhance the number of choices."[1]

Relating these ideas to the challenges above, I see two corresponding imperatives:

1. Architects should solve problems *with* people instead of *for* them by helping them understand their needs and the choices of designs that meet those needs. This is done

by bringing those who use the buildings into the process of designing those buildings.
2. Architects need to better understand science and how much it has in common with architecture. Jacob Bronowski pointed out that the creative scientist is more interested in exploring and expanding ideas than in establishing fixed "truths." The unique quality of human beings lies in the increase rather than the decrease of diversity.

Within this context, sketches can contribute to design, first by facilitating the exploration and diversity of each designer's thinking. Secondly, sketches can help open up the design process by developing communication *with* people instead of presenting conclusions *to* people.

The notion of *graphic thinking* grew out of the recognition that sketching or drawing can and should support the designer's thinking. I realize that some readers would be more comfortable with a book about either thinking or drawing, but I felt it was critical to deal with their interaction. Pulling them apart seemed to be like trying to understand how a fish swims by studying the fish and the water separately. I hope you will be able to bear with the rough spots in this book and find some things that will help in your work.

Acknowledgments

This book is dedicated to those architects who generously took time to discuss their use of drawings in design while I was completing my research; many of whom also provided sketches to illustrate the text. Their dedication to creativity in architecture, enthusiasm for drawing, and comments about their design processes were a great help and inspiration for my work. Among these architects I am especially indebted to David Stieglitz, Thomas Beeby, Morse Payne, Thomas Larson, Michael Gebhart, Romaldo Giurgola, James Tice and Norman Crowe.

Recognition is due the following people for their particularly important contributions to this effort:

Robert McKim—for his insights to visual thinking and his encouragement.
Susan Lewis—for very valuable criticism about communicating my ideas.
Jim Anderson—for vital comments on graphic communication.

Alberta Gordon—for steering the book through production.
Danielle Ponsolle—for her fine efforts to make the text readable.

Jack Wyman, Ken Carpenter, Juan Bonta, Charles Sappenfield and my other colleagues at the College of Architecture and Planning, Ball State University —for comments and moral support.
Larry Hager—for believing in the book.
Fuller Moore—for first suggesting the book.

A special thanks to Forrest Wilson for his continuing and enthusiastic support.

Finally thanks must be given to my wife Peggy and children, Michele, Kevin, and Madeleine for their great patience and sacrifices while I was chained to the typewriter.

Previously published drawings photographed by Jerry Hoffman.

Contents

GRAPHIC THINKING FOR ARCHITECTS AND DESIGNERS

1 Introduction

Graphic Thinking is a term I have adopted to describe thinking assisted by sketching. In architecture, this type of thinking is usually associated with the conceptual design stages of a project in which thinking and sketching work closely together as stimulants for developing ideas. Interest in this form of thinking is promoted by a reexamination of the history of architectural design, the impact of visual communication in society and new concepts of the role of design and designers.

There is actually a very strong tradition in architecture for graphic thinking. Looking through reproductions of the notebooks of Leonardo da Vinci, we are struck by the dynamic thinking which they reflect. It is impossible to really understand or appreciate da Vinci's thinking apart from his drawings because the graphic images and the thinking are one, a unity. A closer look at these sketches reveals certain features which are instructive for anyone interested in graphic thinking.

1. There are many different ideas on one page; his attention is constantly shifting from one subject to another.
2. The way da Vinci looks at problems is diverse both in method and in scale; there

are often perspectives, sections, plans, details, and panoramic views on the same page.
3. The thinking is exploratory, open-ended; the sketches are loose and fragmented, while showing how they were derived. Many alternatives for extending the ideas are suggested. The spectator is invited to participate.

What a marvelous example! Here is a mind in ferment, using drawings as a means of discovery rather than a way to impress other people.

Although it is often difficult to find records of developmental sketches in historical documents, there is enough surviving evidence to inducate that the use of sketches for thinking was common to architects throughout history. Depending on the dictates of the building trades or customs, the drawing conventions varied from plan to section to elevation. For almost two centuries, the Ecole des Beaux Arts in Paris utilized the plan "esquisse" as the

1

foundation for its training method. With the establishment of large architectural firms in the United States, three-dimensional, scale models gradually replace drawing for the purposes of development of designs. The use of designing sketches further declined with the advent of the professional model makers and professional renderers.

There has, of course, been an intense interest in architect's drawings rekindled by exhibits like the Beaux Arts and 200 Years of American Architectural Drawings. But the emphasis is mostly on communication of the final fixed product and these presentation drawings tell us practically nothing about the way in which the buildings were designed. The thinking sketches are necessary to understand the step by step process. Yet even when the thinking sketches are available, as in the documents of the work of LeCorbusier, they usually over-looked in favor of the renderings or photos of the finished work. We are just beginning to appreciate more LeCorbusier's abilities through his sketches.

"All the internal harmony of the work is in the drawings . . . It is incredible that artists today should be indifferent (even hostile) to this prime mover, this 'scaffolding' of the project."[1]

1–6 By Norman Jaffe·

1–7 By Thomas Beeby. House of Virgil

Among modern architects, Alvar Aalto has probably left us one of the best models of the graphic thinking tradition. His sketches are rapid and diverse; they deftly probe the subject. Hand, eye, and mind are intensely concentrated. The sketches record the level of development, proficiency, and clarity of Aalto's ideas. There are many other architects whose work we can turn to, particularly here, in the United States, where we are experiencing a resurgence of sketching. Their drawings are inventive, diverse and provocative. Whether they are making notes in a sketchbook or turning over concepts in the design studio, these creative designers are looking for something special over and above solving the design problem, like the gourmet who is looking for something more than food. They enjoy the "eureka" experience and they enjoy the search as well. This book is really about finding things, about seeing new ideas, about discovery and about sharing ideas and discoveries.

VISUAL COMMUNICATION
THROUGH TIME

Throughout history, vision has had an important impact on thinking. Starting with the caveman, drawings were a way of "freezing" ideas and events outside of himself and creating a history. In many ways, the "second world" which man created through his images was critical to the evolution of thinking. Man was able to separate the here-and-now from what could be imagined, a future. Through images the world of the spirit, the ideal world of mythology, and compelling utopias became immediate and real. The ideals of an entire culture could be contained in one picture; the unspeakable could be shared with others. From earliest times, this visual expression of thinking has been communal. Once a concept, such as the notion of man being able to fly, was converted to an image, it was free to be reinterpreted again and again by others until the plane was invented.

Man used signs and symbols long before written languages were adopted. Early written languages, as Egyptian hieroglyphics, were highly specialized sets of symbols derived from pictures. The development of geometry, combining mathematics with diagrams, made it possible to think of structure and other abstractions of reality. This lead to the construction of objects or buildings of monumental scale from designs. In addition to trying to make sense of his immediate surroundings, man used drawings to reach out into the unknown. Maps reconstituted from notes and sketches of explorers sparked the imagination and stimulated new discoveries about our world and the universe.

In spite of the ascendency of written language, visual communication continues to be an essential part of the way we think. This is revealed in these phrases that liberally sprinkle our everyday conversation: "I see what you mean; take another look at the situation; put this all in perspective." Although research opinion varies, it seems generally accepted that 70 to 80 percent of what we learn is through sight. Sight seems to be the most rapid and comprehensive of our senses for receiving information. Through centuries of conditioning, we rely on vision as an early warning of danger. Not only have we come to depend on sight as a primary means of understanding the world, we have also learned to translate information picked up by the senses into visual clues, so that, in many ways, sight is actually used as a substitute for the other senses.

There is sample evidence that visual communication is becoming an even more powerful force in our lives. The most obvious example is television through which we can explore the skies, the oceans and the societies of our shrinking planet. We rely heavily on graphics explain and persuade. Cartoons have become a very sophisticated means of distilling and reflecting our culture. But the most significant revolution is the move of visual communication from the realm of the specialists to the grasp of the general public. Instantly developing film and video recorders are just the beginning of the visual tools that will become as common as the typewriter and the calculator.

The potential of visual communication will be tested as we approach the twenty-first century. Two overriding features are the deluge of information that we must absorb and the increasing interactive nature of the problems we must solve. As Edward Hamilton put it, "Up . . . to the present age we have absorbed information in a one-thing-at-a-time, an abstract, linear, fragmented but sequential way . . . . Now, the term, pattern, . . . will apply increasingly in understanding the world of total-environmental stimuli into which we are moving."[2] We seek patterns, not only to screen for significance of information, but also to illustrate processes or structures by which our world operates. The emerging technology for collecting, storing, and displaying different models of reality hold exciting promise. Computer constructed satellite maps, video games, computer graphics, and the miniaturization of computing and recording equipment will open up a new era in visual communication.

The full utilization of this new capability will be directly related to the development of our own visual thinking. "Computers cannot see or dream, nor can they create: computers are language-bound. Similarly, thinkers who cannot escape the structure of language, who are unaware that thinking can occur in ways having little to do with language, are often utilizing only a small part of their brain that is indeed like a computer."[3] This observation by Robert McKim points out the critical issue of man-machine interaction. The new equipment is of no value in itself; it is only as good as our imagination can make it. If we are to realize the potential of visual technology, we must learn to *think visually*.

VISUAL THINKING

The study of visual thinking has developed in a major part from the study of creativity within the field of psychology. The work of Rudolph Arnheim, in the psychology of art, has been particularly significant. In his book, *Visual Thinking,* he laid a basic framework for research by dissolving the artifical barrier between thinking and the action of the senses. "By cognitive, I mean all mental operations involved in receiving, storing, and processing of information: sensory perception, memory, thinking, learning."[4] This was a new way of understanding perception, namely an integration of mind and senses; the focus of the study of creativity shifts from the mind or the senses to the interaction of both.

Visual thinking is therefore a form of thinking which utilizes the products of vision—seeing, imagining, and drawing. Within the context of designing, the focus of this book will be on the third product of vision, drawings or sketches. When thinking becomes externalized in the form of a sketched image, it can be said to have become *graphic.*

There are strong indications that thinking in any field is greatly enhanced by the use of more than one sense as in doing while seeing. Although this book's focus is on architectural design, it is my hope that other readers will find the explanations and examples useful. The long history of architectural design has produced a great wealth of graphic techniques and imagery in response to high complex, comprehensive, quantitative-qualitative problems. Today, architectural design attempts to deal with our total man-made environment, a problem which is personal and pressing for everyone. The graphic thinking tools used by architects to solve problems of interaction, conflict, efficiency, and aesthetics in buildings have now become important to all parts of society with its own increasingly complex problems.

GRAPHIC THINKING:
A COMMUNICATION PROCESS

The process of graphic thinking can be seen as a conversation with ourselves in which we communicate with sketches. The communication process involves the sketched image on the paper, the eye, the brain, and the hand. How can this apparently closed network generate ideas that are not already in the brain? Part of the answer lies in the definition of an idea. The so-called "new ideas" are really a new way of looking at and combining old ideas. All ideas can be said to be connected; the thinking process reshuffles ideas, focuses on parts and recombines them. In the diagram of the graphic thinking process all four parts—eye, brain, hand, and sketch have the capability to add, subtract, or modify the information that is being passed through the communication loop. The eye, assisted by perception, can select a focal point and screen out other information (for a discussion of perception, see the Appendix). We can readily accept that the brain can add information. But the other two parts, hand and sketch, are also important to the process. A difference often exists between what we intend to draw and what actually is drawn. Drawing ability, materials, our mood can all be sources of change. And yes, even the image on paper is subject to change. Differences in light intensity and angle, the size and distance of the image from the eye, reflectancy of paper and transparency of media all open up new possibilities.

The potential of graphic thinking lies in the continuous cycling of information from paper to eye to brain to hand and back to the paper. Theoretically, the more often the information is passed around the loop, the more opportunities for change. In this illustration, for example,

Image on Paper

Perceptual Image

Mental Image

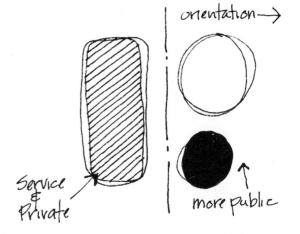

I started with a sketch of cartoon-like bubbles to represent spaces in a house that is yet to be designed. Depending on my experience, interests, and what I am trying to do, I will see certain things in the sketch and ignore others. The resulting perceptual image segregates special-use spaces, the living room and kitchen, from several other more private or support spaces. Next, I form a mental image to further organize the spaces and give them orientation based on what I already know about the site or a southern exposure for the living room and kitchen. When this mental image is transferred to paper once more, it goes through yet another change in which the special spaces begin to take on distinctive forms.

This is, of course, an oversimplification of the process. Graphic thinking, like visual communication with the real world, is a continuous process. Information is simultaneously darting all over the network. When graphic thinking is most active, it is similar to watching a fantastic array of fireworks, looking for the one you really enjoy. Not only is it productive, it is fun. "Far from being a passive mechanism of registration like the photographic camera, our visual apparatus copes with the incoming images in active struggle."[5] Visual thinking and visual perception cannot be separated from other types of thinking or perception. Verbal thinking, for example, adds more to the idea of a kitchen or living room with such quali-

fiers as bright, open, or comfortable. Obviously, graphic thinking is not all you need to know in order to solve problems or think creatively but it can be a basic tool. Graphic thinking can open up channels of communication with ourselves and those people with whom we work. The sketches generated are important because they show *how* we are thinking about a problem, not just *what* we think about it.

Graphic thinking takes advantage of the power of visual perception by making visual images external and explicit. By putting them on paper, we give visual images an objectivity outside our brain, an existence of their own

New Image on Paper

special shape responding to interior & exterior uses.

simplified order for the kitchen

Multiple Messages

over time. Graphic thinking, as externalized thinking, "has several advantages over internalized thought. First, direct sensory involvement with materials provides sensory nourishment—literally 'food for thought.' Second, thinking by manipulating an actual structure permits serendipity—the happy accident, the unexpected discovery. Third, thinking in the direct context of sight, touch, and motion engenders a sense of immediacy, actuality and action. Finally, the externalized thought structure provides an object for critical contemplation as well as a visible form that can be shared with a colleague . . ."[7] To the person who must regularly seek new solutions to problems, who must think creatively, these qualities of immediacy, stimulation, accident and contemplation are very important. To these qualities I would add one more special attribute of graphic thinking, simultaneity. Sketches allow us to see a great amount of information at the same time, exposing relationships and describing a wide range of subtleties. Sketches are direct and representative. "The power of visual language lies in its spontaneous evidence, its almost childlike simplicity. . . . Darkness means darkness, things that belong together are shown together, and what is great and high appears in large size and in a high location."[8]

1–23a   By David Stieglitz. Development sketches on back of a placemat, Siegler Residence.

1–23 b   Front of placemat, Hotel Mercur, Copenhagen

A standard story that many architects delight in telling describes how the most basic concept for a multimillion-dollar project was first scribbled on the back of a restaurant napkin. I have wondered why both, the teller and the listener, always seem to derive amusement from such a story. Perhaps the story restores confidence in the strength of the individual designer, or maybe it is the incongruity that decisions on such important matters are being made in such a relaxed, casual manner. Viewing this story in the context of graphic thinking, it is not at all surprising that inspired, inventive thinking should take place at a restaurant table. Not only are the eyes, minds, and hands of at least two persons interacting with the images on the napkin, but they are further stimulated by conversation. Besides, these persons are separated from their day to day work problems; they are relaxing in a pleasant atmosphere and with the consumption of, one hopes, good food, their level of anxiety is significantly reduced. They are open, ready, prepared for discovery; indeed, it would only be surprising if the most furtive ideas were *not* born in this setting.

To be an effective communicator, an architect must:

1. Understand the basic elements of communication—the communicator, the receiver or audience, the media, and the context—and their role in effectiveness.
2. Develop a graphic language from which to draw the most effective sketches for specific communication tasks.
3. Never take for granted the process of communication and be willing to take the time to examine his own effectiveness.

MEDIA

RECEIVER

COMMUNICATOR

CONTEXT

Basic communication theory stresses the communication loop between the communicator or sender and the receiver in order to attain maximum effectiveness. Response from the audience is essential to a speaker who wants to get his message across. The information coming from the receiver is as important as what the sender, the architect transmits. And so, we must pay very close attention to those persons with whom we hope to communicate. The best approach is to try to place yourself in their shoes. What are they expecting? What are their concerns? Equally important, we should be aware of our motivations and concerns. Do we have an unconscious or hidden agenda?

As further chapters review the many ways graphic thinking is used in the practice of architecture, it is critical to remember that individuals cannot really be cut away from their environment or their society. The graphic thinking of one person thrives in the presence of good company and a supportive atmosphere. Seek both enthusiastically.

Although the medium with which this book deals is principally freehand sketches, the basic methods are applicable to many graphic media. But each specific medium has some unique characteristics which will have special effect on communication. Experimentation

with different media is the fastest route to using them effectively. Although there are books on the use of these media, there is no substitute for practice because we all have different needs and abilities.

The context for communication includes such things as location, time, duration, weather, type of space, what took place before the communication, what will take place after. We may be able to control some of these context variables, but we cannot afford to ignore them.

13

1-25   Gym, St. Mary's College, C. F. Murphy
        Associates, Architects

1-26   Wall section, Headquarters Building, Smith,
        Hinchman & Grylls Associates, Inc.

THE ROLE OF GRAPHIC THINKING IN ARCHITECTURE

To realize the potential of graphic thinking in architecture, we must understand today's prevailing attitudes on the design process and the use of drawings in that process. In the early nineteen sixties, A. S. Levens was able to write with confidence that, "One source of confusion in thinking about design is the tendency to identify design with one of its languages, drawing. This fallacy is similar to the confusion which would result if musical composition were to be identified with the writing of notes on a staff of five lines, Design, like musical composition, is done essentially in the mind and the making of drawings or writing of notes is a recording process."[6] Today, we have broader concept of how and where design takes place, but drawings are still normally thought of as simple *representations* of ideas; their purpose is to explain to other people the *products* of our thinking, the conclusions. Training in architectural schools has been primarily geared toward the attainment of finished presentation skills while in architectural offices, the emphasis has been on turning out working drawings which clearly present the necessary directives for the contractors.

In response to Levens' analogy, graphic thinking treats drawings more like a piano than a score sheet. Like composition, design is possible without an instrument to provide feedback but for most designers this is not too productive. Design thinking and design communication should be interactive; this implies new roles for graphics.

14

ORGANIZATION OF THE BOOK

The first and major part of the book is devoted to basic graphic thinking skills and their role in design thinking. In study and practice I have identified six main uses of graphic thinking in architectural design:

representation   discovery
abstraction   verification
manipulation   stimulation

Although there are some obvious applications of these uses to a number of design process models, I have purposely avoided stressing such links. One of the problems with design process models is their acceptance in too simplistic a way; types of thinking or behavior are categorized and the intermeshing of processes and ideas is ignored. Instead of categories, we need flexibility. Manipulation of graphic images, for example, might be used at many stages of designing. I still would not attempt to guess where it will be handy for a specific project: Manipulation of the stereotypes for a building could get designing started; distortion of an elevation might reveal a new approach to detailing; reversal of a process diagram might suggest a modification of the building program.

The second part of this book looks at the implications of graphic thinking for architectural design on three scales:

individual design
team design
public design

The emphasis is on better communication so that ideas can be shared. The following is a collection of images, ideas, and devices which I hope are helpful and enjoyable. The approach is eclectic rather than discriminating, inclusive not exclusive, expectant not conclusive. The intent is not simply to describe examples but to convey the excitement of graphic thinking and even make it contagious. We all have special, unique capacities for thinking, which, if unlocked, could make great contributions to the solution of problems we face. "Every great artist gives birth to a new universe, in which the familiar things look the way they have never before looked to anyone."[9] This book is written in anticipation of a time when many of us will be able to give birth to our own "universe."

Part I
Graphic Thinking Processes

Dark
green

Canopy
of
Trees

Red

Shaded
lawn

Brick
walk

2 Basic Skills

This chapter's focus is on the basic skills helpful to graphic thinking methods as presented in the remainder of this book. Developing freehand drawing skills is necessary to the attainment of graphic thinking and perceptual skills. Some might say "I really admire good drawings and those designers who have a quick hand, but I have accepted the fact that I will never be that good." Bunk! It just is not so! *Anyone* can learn to draw well. If you don't believe me, take the time to talk to people who draw very well. You will find that their first drawings were tentative. They probably took every opportunity to draw. With time and hard work, they gradually improved and never regretted the effort they made.

There are two important conditions to keep in mind when trying to develop any skill:

1. Skill comes with repetition
2. The surest way to practice any skill is to enjoy what you are doing.

Because of the heavy emphasis on rationalization in formal education, many people mistakenly think that they can master a skill, such as drawing, simply by understanding concepts. Concepts are helpful but practice is essential.

Artie Shaw, the orchestra conductor, once explained why he refused all requests by parents to audition their children. He felt that the worst thing that you can do to a talented child is to tell him he has talent. The 'greats' in the music business, regardless of natural talent, became successful with hard work and a commitment to their craft. They believed in themselves, but knew they would have to struggle to prove it to others. The focus of energy, sense of competition, and years of hard work are essential to their becoming fine musicians.

The knowledge that drawing and thinking are important to architecture is not sufficient. Natural drawing talent is not enough. To sustain the necessary lifetime effort of learning and perfecting graphic thinking, we need to find pleasure in drawing and thinking. We must be challenged to do it better than those architects we admire. Morse Payne of The Architects Collaborative noted the influence of Ralph Rapsin on many talented designers, "To watch Ralph knock out one of his beautiful perspectives in fifteen minutes was truly inspiring. It set a goal for us that was very challenging."[1] Fortunately, there is still a lot of respect within the architectural profession for high quality drawing. The person who can express himself graphically as well as verbally, on an impromptu basis, is highly valued. When hiring, offices often look for ability to communicate over ability to be original. They know that your ability to develop ideas *with* them is much more important in the long run than the ideas you initially bring *to* them.

One last note—it is possible to be an architect without having well-developed graphic thinking skills. A barber or a bartender can surely cut hair or serve drinks without being able to carry on a conversation. But the job is a lot easier if you enjoy talking with people and you will probably do more business. I believe that graphic thinking can make design more enjoyable and more effective.

FREEHAND DRAWING AS A BASIC TOOL

The thousands of students who pass through
architectural schools are usually told that they
should learn to sketch freehand and, to a
certain degree how. Rarely are they told what
they should sketch or why. Drawing cubes
or other still-life exercises try to teach sketching divorced from thinking. Most students
find it boring and it drives some away from
sketching for the rest of their lives. I prefer to
start students with the sketching of existing
buildings because:

1. They are drawing subjects in which they
   have a basic interest and are ready to
   discuss.
2. The eye and mind as well as the hand are
   involved; perception becomes fine-tuned
   and we begin to sort out our visual experiences.
3. One of the best ways to learn about archi-

tectural design is to look closely at existing
buildings and spaces.

The clearest way to demonstrate the value of
freehand sketching for developing graphic
thinking skills is to compare sketching with
photography. Although a camera is often
a useful or expedient tool, it lacks many of
the attributes of sketches. Sketches have the
ability to reveal our perception, therefore
giving more importance to certain parts whereas a photo shows everything with equal emphasis. In the above sketch of the Spanish
Steps in Rome, the focus is on the church,

ellipse and steps as organizing elements for the
entire exterior space. The significant impact
of the flowers in the photo has been eliminated
in the sketch. The abstraction can be pushed
further until there is only a pattern of light
and dark or we can focus in on only certain
details as lamp posts or windows. This one
scene alone is a *dictionary* of urban design.
But you do not have to wait till you get to
Rome in order to get started; there are lessons
all around us. Become a prospector of architectural design; build your own collection
of good ideas while you learn to sketch. It is a
lot of fun.

2-4   Window detail

2-5   Street lamp detail

Line / Structure

Tones

BUILDING A SKETCH

In his book *Drawing Buildings,* Richard
Downer presented the most effective approach
to freehand sketching I have ever come across.
"The first and most important thing about
drawing buildings is to realize that what you
intend to draw should interest you as a subject."[2] Next, it is important to select a vantage
point which best describes your subject. Now
you are ready to build the sketch by a three-
step process of sketching basic structure, tones,
and then details. The basic structure sketch
is most important. If the parts are not shown
in their proper place and correct proportions
it makes no difference what is drawn from
then on, the sketch will always look wrong. So
take your time; look carefully at the subject;
continually compare your sketch with what
you see. Now add the tones. These represent
the space-defining elements of light, shadow,
and color. Again, look carefully at the subject.
Where are the lightest tones; where are the
darkest? The sketch is becoming more realistic.
The details are added on last. At this point
everything is in its place and you can really
concentrate on the details one at a time. It is
no longer overwhelming; you can relax and
enjoy it.

Texture/Color

Detail

Basic Structure Sketch

The most important part of a sketch, the basic line drawing, is also the most difficult skill to master. It requires a lot of practice but I have found a few suggestions that should help:

1. To help sharpen the sense of proportion needed for sketching, practice drawing squares and then rectangles two or three times longer on one side than on the other. Now try to find squares in a scene you are sketching. (At the beginning, this could be done with tracing paper over a photograph.)

2. Use a cross or a frame to get the parts of the sketch in their proper place or maybe a prominent feature of the scene or subject can act as an organizer for the other parts of the sketch.

3. Although pencil can certainly be used for sketching, I prefer felt-tip or ink pens because the lines they produce are simple and clear. If a line is in the wrong place, it is quite evident. Since the line can not be erased, it must be redrawn to get it right. This process of repetition and checking against the subject develops skill. Drawings which are so light that they can be ignored

or which can be erased, deny the designer the feedback which is essential to his improvement.

4. To gain more control over line-making, try some simple exercises similar to our "idle moment" doodles. The spirals, like those above, are drawn from the outside toward the center, both clockwise and counterclockwise. Try to make them as fast as possible without letting the lines touch each other; try to get the lines close to each other. Straight hatching can be done in several directions always striving for consistency.

Tones

Tones can be represented with different densities or combinations of cross-hatching. The lines should be parallel and have equal spaces between them. Always remember that the main purpose of the cross-hatching is to obtain different levels of grey or darkness. Use straight strokes as if you were painting the surfaces with a brush. Erratic or irregular lines draw attention to themselves and distract the eye from more important things. There is no strict rule to applying tones on a sketch, but I have some preferences which seem to work well. Horizontal hatching is used on horizontal surfaces, diagonal hatching on vertical surfaces. When two vertical surfaces meet the hatching on one is at a slightly different angle from the hatching on the other surface.

Apply tones in a three-step process: 1. indicate any texture that appears in the surface such as the vertical boards on a barn; 2. if the texture indication does not provide the level of darkness of the subject, add the necessary additional hatching over the entire surface; 3. now apply more hatching where any shadows fall. To show gradations of shadow, add a succession of hatches at different angles. The refinement of tones in a drawing is achieved by looking carefully at the subject and by getting more control over the consistency of the lines.

A number of alternative techniques for sketching in tones are illustrated throughout this book. The one shown above is a rapid method using random strokes. Each designer usually develops techniques with which he feels most comfortable.

Details

Details are often the most interesting or compelling aspect of buildings. The window is an excellent example. There, the details can be the result of a transition between two materials—brick and glass or between two building elements—wall and opening. The wood window frame, the brick arch, keystone and window sill make these transitions possible and each of these details tell us more about the building. On a regular basis, I have students sketch windows, doors, or other building elements so they gain an understanding and appreciation

of the contribution of details to the qualities and functions of the building. Details tell us something of needs and materials as well as our ingenuity in relating them. The sketch of the metal grating around the base of the tree explains both the needs of the tree and the use of the surface under the tree where people walk.

In most architectural scenes, there are details which are close to us and others further away. We can see more of the close detail and should show in the sketch such things as screws or fasteners or fine joints and textures. As details

recede in the sketch, fewer and fewer of the pieces are shown until only the outline is visible.

2-18   By Ronald Margolis. Old Main Building,
       Wayne University

2-19   By Lawrence Halprin

2-20   By Karl Mang

old parsh quarter...

THE SKETCH-NOTEBOOK

"People who look at things without seeing them, will experience the same deficiency when calling up mental pictures, while those who . . . look at things squarely and with recognition will have an equally alert internal eye."[3] Visual imagery is critical to the creative designer; he must rely on a very rich collection of visual memories. The richness of these memories depends on a well-developed and active visual perception. The sketch-notebook is an excellent way of collecting visual images and sharpening perception for it promotes seeing rather than just looking. Architects who have gotten into the sketch-notebook habit quickly discover its usefulness. All I can say is try it and you'll like it.

A sketch-notebook should be small and portable, able to fit into a pocket so it can be carried anywhere. It should have a durable binding and covers so it won't come apart. Carry it with you at all times and leave it next to your bed at night (some of the best ideas come to people just before going to sleep or right upon awakening). As the name implies, it is a book for notes as well as for sketches and for reminders, recipes or anything else you can think about. Combining verbal and graphic notes will help unite verbal and visual thinking. (see illustration of pages in architects' sketchbooks).

Chichicastenango, Guatemala, 1972

CHICHICASTENANGO
69. 6.2.72 R

Many architects have become methodical about sketch and note taking. Gordon Cullen, the British illustrator and urban design consultant, has had a major influence in the use of analytical sketches. His book *Townscape*[4] is a wonderful collection of visual perceptions of urban environment. The sketches are clear and comprehensive, impressive evidence of what can be discovered with graphic thinking. Using plans, sections, and perspectives, the sketches go beyond the obvious to uncover new perceptions. Tones are used to identify major organizers of space. (In the book, many of these tones are achieved mechanically but they are easily rendered in sketches by hatching with grease pencil or large felt-tip markers.) The verbal categorization of urban phenomena through short titles helps to fix the visual perceptions in our memories; verbal and graphic communication are working together. And these are not complicated sketches; they

Outdoor cafe arcade

Main Pedestrian street

are within the potential of most designers, as shown in the sketches above which apply Cullen's techniques to the analysis of a small midwestern town.

"A sketchbook should be a personal diary of what interests you and not a collection of finished drawings compiled to impress with weight and number . . . a finished on-the-spot drawing . . . shouldn't be the reason you go out, for the objective is *drawing* and not *the drawing.* I often learn more from drawings that don't work out, studying the unsuccessful attempts to see where and why I went off. I can learn more . . . than from a drawing where everything fell into place. . . . The drawings that succeed do so in some measure because of the failures I've learned from preceding it, and so certain pitfalls were unconsciously ignored while drawing."[5]

2-24   Cartoon style sketch, after Rowland Wilson

2-25a   Original sketch
2-25b   Overlay sketch
2-25c   Final sketch
2-26a   Original sketch
2-26b   Enlargement of sketch

CARTOONS

Cartoons are an important source of sketching
ideas. My favorite sources are the New Yorker
and Punch magazines but there are many
other sources. Cartoonists convey a convincing
sense of reality with an incredible economy
of means. Simple contour lines suggest detail
information while concentrating on overall
shapes. Michael Folkes, describes some of the
discipline of cartoon drawings, ''. . . simplicity
refers to the need to make the clearest possible
statement . . . Avoid all unnecessary detail.
Make the focal point of your picture stand out.
Refrain from filling every corner with objects
or shading. . . . Train your hand and eye to
put down on paper rapidly recognizable
situations . . . in the fewest possible strokes.
One significant detail is worth far more than an
uncertain clutter of lines that don't really
describe anything. Make dozens of small pictures . . . drawing directly in pen and ink so
that the pen becomes a natural drawing instrument and not something that can only be
used to work painfully over carefully prepared
pencil lines.''[6]

TRACING

Tracing existing graphic material is another way of building sketching skills. Making an overlay of your own drawings with tracing paper is an obvious but under-used device. Rather than overwork a drawing that is headed in the wrong direction, make an overlay showing the elements that need to be corrected and then in another overlay, make a whole new sketch incorporating the changes. You will learn more from your mistakes and the final sketch will be better and fresher. Tracing can also be done by laying a transparent sheet with a grid over a drawing or photo, drawing a larger grid, and then transfer the drawing square by square. A third technique uses a slide projector and a small mirror to project images of a convenient size for tracing on your drawing table. The large sketch on page 29 was done in this way.

No matter the reason you thought copying was improper or illegal, forget it. Master draftsmen such as Leonardo da Vinci copied other peoples' work when they were learning to draw. No tracing is ever the same as the original. You will pick out some details and simplify other parts. Tracing forces you to look closely at the original sketch or photo and better understand the subject.

zoom lens: not essential
but allows for adjustment
of drawing size.

Small mirror

support
brackets

shelf

about 18"

counter or
drafting board

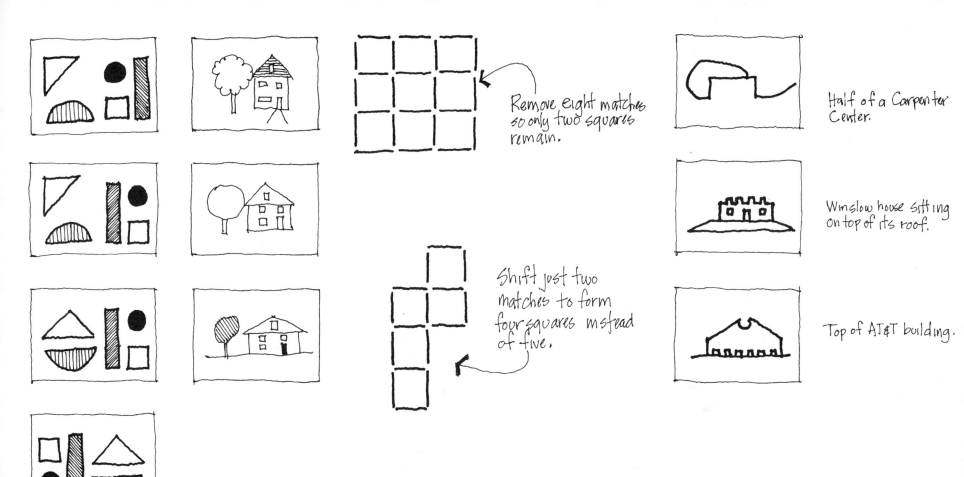

Remove eight matches so only two squares remain.

Shift just two matches to form four squares instead of five.

Half of a Carpenter Center.

Winslow house sitting on top of its roof.

Top of AT&T building.

1. 2. 3. 4.

VISUAL-MENTAL GAMES

An entertaining way to improve hand-eye-mind coordination and promote an ability to visualize is to play some simple games.

1. Show to a couple or more people, four or five cutouts of simple shapes arranged on a piece of paper. Out of view of the others, one person moves the cutouts while describing verbally the move. The other persons attempt to draw the new arrangement from the description. This is repeated a few times to see who can keep track of the position of the shapes.

After mastering this exercise, have the persons drawing try to form a mental picture of each new arrangement and then try to draw only the final arrangement. In a second version of this game, an object is substituted for the cutouts and it is manipulated or opened or taken apart. (2–28)

2. Form a circle with a small group. Each person makes a simple sketch and passes it to his right. Everyone tries to copy the sketch he has received and in turn passes the copy to the right. This continues until the final copy is passed to the source of the original sketch. Then all sketches are arranged on a wall or table in the order

they were made. This game illustrates the distinctiveness of individual visual perception. (2–29)

3. Doodles, using an architectural or design theme, are another form of puzzle. Here, the objective is to provide just enough clues so the subject is obvious once the title is given. (2–30)

There are many visual puzzles which exercise our visual perception. Try some of those shown above; look for more puzzles, or invent some of your own. (2–31)

3 Representation

"Represent: Call up by description or portrayal or imagination, figure, place likeness of before mind or senses, serve or be meant as likeness of . . . , stand for, be specimen of, fill place of, be substitute for . . ."[1]

Throughout history, representation and design have been closely linked. The act of designing grew directly out of the desire of men to see what they could or would achieve before investing too much time, energy or money. To create a clay pot meant simply working directly with your hands until the desired result was achieved. But making a gold pot required expensive material, much preparation, time and energy. A representation, a design drawing, of the gold bowl was necessary before starting the project. Design became an important part of architectural projects simply because of their scale. Representing the imagined building permitted not only a view of the final result but also the planning for labor and materials to assure completion of the project.

The representational capacity of sketches is limited. We must recognize that, even with the most sophisticated techniques, drawings are not a full substitute for the actual experience of an architectural environment. On the other hand, the capacity of sketches as thinking tools extends well beyond what is actually contained in the sketches. Drawings, as representations, should be seen as extensions of the person(s) who uses them to aid in thinking.

"The world of images does not simply imprint itself upon a faithfully sensitive organ. Rather, in looking at an object, we reach out for it. With an invisible finger we move through space around us, go out to distant places where things are found, touch them, catch them, scan their surfaces, trace their borders, explore their texture. It is an eminently active occupation."[2]

I find a great variation in the degree with which architects rely on drawings to visualize designs. One probable explanation for this is experience in visualizing and with the building of these designs. For example when an architectural student looks at a plan view of a room, he likely sees just an abstract diagram, but some experienced architects can visualize a perspective view of the same room without having to draw the perspective.

Some basic types of representation sketches, which I feel architects should be able to understand, will be discussed in this chapter. I do not intend to present a comprehensive explanation of basic drawing. There are already several good books on that subject. Rather, the emphasis will be on freehand techniques without the use of triangles, scales, and straight edges allowing for rapid representation. There are a great number of things we can represent about a space or a building and many ways to represent them. The sketched subjects can range in scale from a building and its surrounding property to a window or a light switch. We might be interested in how it looks or how it works or how to put it together; we may be searching for clarity or character.

Variations in drawings range from the concrete to the abstract, and the conventions include section or cut, elevation, perspective, axonometric, isometric, and projections. Media, technique, and style account for many of the other variations. Many of these variations will be covered in later chapters.

The elementary forms of representation discussed at this point are:

1. Comprehensive views—In order to study designs as complete systems, we must have models which represent the whole from *some* viewpoint.

2. Concrete images—Dealing with the most direct experience. Abstraction will be covered in the next two chapters.

3. Perceptual focus—Trying to involve the viewer in the experience signified by the drawing.

4. Freehand sketches—Decision-making in design should include the consideration of many alternatives. Representation of alternatives is encouraged by the speed of freehand sketching whereas it is discouraged by the tediousness of "constructed" hardline drawings.

PERSPECTIVE

Perspective sketches have an equal standing with the plan drawings—the starting point of most design education. One-point perspective is the easiest and therefore, I feel, the most useful of perspective conventions. I have found the following three-step method most success-ful:

1. Indicate the picture-plane in both eleva-tion and plan; it is usually a wall or another feature which defines the far limits of the immediate space to be viewed. Locate

the point from which the space is to be viewed or viewpoint (V.P.). Vertically this point is usually about 5½ feet from the bottom of the picture-plane; horizontally it can be placed just about anywhere in the space with the understanding that parts of the space outside a 60 degree cone of vision in front of the viewer will tend to be distorted in the perspective. The horizontal line drawn through the V.P. is called the horizon line.

2. Establish a grid on the floor of the space. Draw the square grid in plan and count the

number of spaces the viewer is away from the picture-plane. Then, in the perspective, locate the diagonal-vanishing-point (D.V.P.) on the horizon line at the same distance from the viewpoint. Draw floor grid lines in the perspective in one direction coming from the viewpoint; draw a diagonal line from the diagonal vanishing-point through the bottom corner of the picture-plane and across the space. Where the diagonal intersects the floor grid lines running in the one direction, horizontal lines can be drawn to show the other direction of the floor grid.

3.

3. Indicate the structure of the basic elements of the space. Continue the grid on the walls and ceiling (if appropriate); using the grids as quick reference, place vertical planes and openings as well as significant divisions of the planes.

Sketching straight lines freehand is an important skill to master for all types of graphic thinking and practice makes perfect. Once you rely on a straight edge, the work slows down. Start by concentrating on where the line begins and ends rather than on the line itself. Place a dot at the beginning and a dot where the line should end. As you repeat this exercise let the pen drag across the paper between the two dots. This sounds pretty elementary but it is surprising how many people have never bothered to learn how to sketch a straight line.

With the basic perspective and plan completed, the values or tones can now be added. The actual color of objects or planes, shade, or shadows can cause differences in values; indication of these changing values shows the interaction of light with the space providing spatial definition. Conventions for casting shadows will be presented when plan drawings are discussed. For now, it is enough to note that shadows are first cast in plan and then added to the perspective using the square grid as a reference. Shade appears on objects on the side opposite to the sun or other source of light where no direct light falls; shaded surfaces are generally lighter in tone than shadows. As in sketching existing buildings, I prefer to use parallel hatch lines to show tones (see Building a Sketch in the preceding chapter).

Finally, details and objects can be added. People are most important because they establish the scale of the space and involve the viewer through an identification with these sketched figures. Simplicity, realistic proportions, and a sense of movement are basic to good human figures such as these. The square grids help in coordinating the placement of human figures and other objects in plan and perspective. Be sure to place people and objects where they would really be; the purpose of the sketch is understanding of the space not camouflaging it.

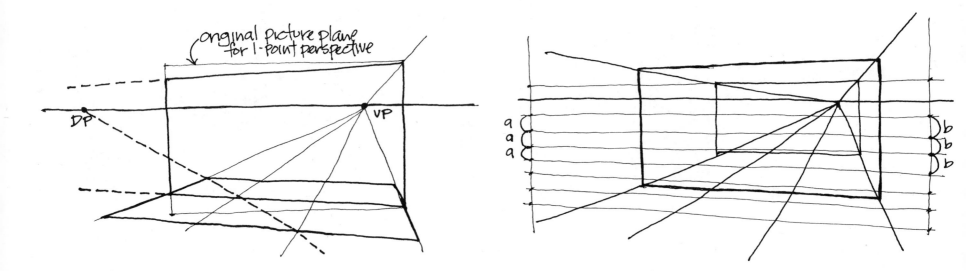

QUALITATIVE REPRESENTATION

At this point we are not interested in the qualities, such as style or technique of the drawing; this will be covered in the chapter on Stimulation. By qualitative representation, I mean the representation of the qualities of a space. "Perspectives are more qualitative than quantitative. The experiential qualities of an environment or object can be perceived directly from a perspective. . . . The qualities of the space/time/light continuum are much better represented and understood in perspective

(than by other conventions)."[3]   In his book *Design Drawing,* William Lockhard makes a very convincing argument for the superiority of perspectives as representational drawings. Perspectives have the advantage of showing the relationship of all the elements of a space in a way most similar to how we would experience it when built. While it is true that buildings are not experienced only through perspectives, it is the best way of showing a direct visual experience of a specific space.

Lockhard's chapter on Representation has probably the best explanation of the use of perspective sketches for representation. Lockhard illustrates a perspective view which is close to one-point perspective; it involves an imaginary second perspective point added at some distance from the sketch (see illustration). Lines running the width of the one-point perspective, parallel with the horizon line, are now slightly slanted in the direction of the imaginary second point. To make the

40

transition from one-point perspective, the top and bottom lines of the picture plane can be given a slight slant and a new plane is established; by drawing a new diagonal, the new diagonal vanishing point can be set. A grid can also be applied to this type perspective to help in placing objects in the space.

To represent the qualities of an imagined space, we have to know something about the qualities of spaces. Though this seems obvious, it is often ignored. As architects, we have to look for what gives spaces their special character; the different kinds of light, color, texture, pattern, or shapes possible and how they are combined. Continual sketching in a sketchnotebook is one sure way of learning about the qualities of spaces. When this knowledge is applied to the representative perspective, we must remember to convey the three-dimensional experience of the space onto a two-dimensional surface, the paper. To do this, we need to illustrate the effects of depth or distance upon those things which give the space its qualities. With an increase in depth, light seems to produce fewer gradations of tone; detail is less evident; texture and color are less vivid; outlines or edges are less sharp. Depth can also be conveyed through overlap of object or contour.

3-16   By Helmut Jacoby. Ford Foundation
        Headquarters, Dinkerloo and Roche, Architects

3-17   By Helmut Jacoby. Boston Government Service
        Center, Paul Rudolph, coordinating architect

SKETCH TECHNIQUES

Many architects have developed their own
sketching styles in an attempt to quickly
represent structure, tones and detail with a
minimum of effort. An especially effective
technique is that of Helmut Jacoby, an architectural delineator of international reputation.
The quick preliminary studies he uses to plan
the final renderings provide remarkable clarity
of spatial definition with an economy of
means. Notice how, with a range of tight and
loose squiggly lines he can define surfaces and
the rapid way he suggests people, trees, textures and other details. The underlying structure of the sketch is usually quite simple with
white areas used to help define space and
objects. Jacoby is very aware of variations in
tone and the effects of shade and shadow with
respect to the surrounding trees as well as
the building.

Michael Gebhardt sketches with an emphasis
on tones and textures, defining space more
through contrasts than line work. With a
looping stroke he is able to establish a consistency which pulls the drawing together and
directs attention to the subject rather than the
media. In establishing your own style, be
sure to examine closely the work of others
that you admire; there is no need to start from
scratch. Also keep in mind that the objective
in sketching is speed and ease.

3-18 By Michael F. Gebhart. Johns–Manville World
Headquarters, The Architects Collaborative

3-19 By Brian Lee. Automatic drawing done without
looking at the paper. It encourages fluidity of
line and naturalness of expression

PLAN SKETCH

Abstract plan diagrams such as the one above have many uses in the early conceptual stages of design. This will be covered in depth in the next chapter. However, many architectural students make the mistake of trying to use these plan diagrams to represent the more concrete decisions about the formation of space. Plan sketches of designed spaces must show what is enclosed and what is not, including scale, height, pattern, and detail. A plan is basically a horizontal cut or section through the space. Things which are cut such as walls or columns are outlined in a heavy line weight. Things which can be seen below the place where the plan was cut are indicated in a lighter line weight. Things such as a skylight which cannot be seen because they are above the level of the cut, can be shown with a heavy dashed line if desired.

The first stage of a representative plan is the heavy outlining of walls clearly showing openings. In the second stage doors, windows, furniture, and other details are added. The third stage sketch includes shadows to show the relative heights of planes and objects. The prevailing convention for shadows casts them on a 45 degree angle, up and to the right. The shadows need only be as long as necessary to clearly show the relative heights of the furniture, walls, etc. Finally color, texture, or pattern can be added to explain further the character of the space.

SECTION

A vertical cut through a space is called a section. What was said about the plan sketch applies also to the section sketch except for the casting of shadows. With sections, we can show depth of space by applying the one-point perspective conventions explained earlier. Imagine you are looking at a cut model of the space; the point at which you look directly into the model is where the viewpoint (V.P.) will be placed. The viewpoint is used to project the perspective behind the section.

Human figures are also important for section sketches. Many designers sketch in view lines for the people; this seems to make it easier to imagine being in the space and gives some sense of what can be seen from a particular position in the space. Shadows can be indicated in order to see the effect of sunlight within the space.

Section Cut line

View or Vanishing Point (VP)

AXONOMETRIC SKETCH

Currently in common use, the axonometric sketch is an important alternative to the perspective, plan, and section. The axonometric is simply a projection from a plan or section in which all parallel lines in the space are shown as parallel; this is in contrast to a perspective where parallel lines are shown as extending from a single point. The axonometric technique is traditional in Chinese drawings. Instead of placing the viewer at a single point from which to view the scene,

it gives the viewer the feeling of being everywhere in front of the scene. The axonometric has the additional advantage of representing three-dimensional space while retaining the "true" dimensions of a plan and section.

This last characteristic makes an axonometric easy to draw since all three dimensions are shown at the same scale. Axonometric projections forward or backward from plans or sections are conventionally made at angles of 30, 45, or 60 degrees but in a sketch the exact angle is not important as long as the projected lines remain parallel.

OTHER REPRESENTATIONS

A variety of sketches based on the conventions of perspective, plan, section, and axonometric are shown on the next two pages. By means of sketches, we can cut open, peel back, pull apart, reconstruct, or make concrete objects transparent in order to see how they are arranged or constructed. These are just a few of the possible extensions of representation. As we use sketches to visualize designs, we should always be ready to invent new tools as needed.

3-23   Plan section, Power Plant enclosure, Grand Coulee
        Dam, Marcel Breuer and Associates, Architects

3-24   By Thomas Truax. Structural systems illustrations,
        Boston City Hall, Kallman, McKinnell & Knowles,
        architects

Designing depends heavily upon representation; to avoid disappointment later, the designer wants to see the physical effects of his decisions. It is inevitable that a student will tell me that he is waiting until he has decided what to do before he draws it up. This is backward. In fact, he cannot decide what to do before he has drawn it. Nine times out of ten indecision is the result of lack of evidence. Furthermore a decision implies a choice; recognizing that there is more than one possible design solution, it makes no sense whatsoever to try to determine if one isolated solution is good. Instead the question should be, is this the best of the known alternatives. To answer this question we must also be able to *see* the other designs. The graphic thinking approach emphasizes sketches which feed thinking and thoughts which feed sketches; one is continually informing the other. For the beginning designer, these points can not be overstressed. There is no way to avoid the intense, comprehensive job of representation or modeling in design. The only choice left is whether or not to make the job easier throughout a professional career by becoming a competent illustrator now.

Having said that, I would add the warning that drawing and thinking must be always open to growth; cliches in drawing lead to cliches in thinking. "I never know what a drawing will look like until it is finished. Once you do— that's security; and security is something we can all do without in a drawing. It comes from working in a particular way or style that enables you to control any subject or situation you encounter, and once you're in control, you stop learning. The nervousness and anxiety that precede a drawing are important to the end result."[5] Architects who have been able to find adventure and excitement in drawing will readily attest to the great boost it gives to their design work and their thinking.

Finally, I want to stress two of my prejudices regarding representative drawing. First, a freehand ability is vital for effective use of representation in architectural design. You must be able to turn over ideas rapidly; to do this requires the spontaneous graphic display that rapid sketching provides. Second, attention should be paid to making the sketches faithfully represent design ideas. Avoid adding things to a drawing simply to improve the appearance of the drawing. Changes should reflect conscious changes in the design. "Remember, the best, most direct and honest persuasion for a design's acceptance should be the design itself, and all successful persuasion should be based on competent and honest representations of the design . . ."[6]

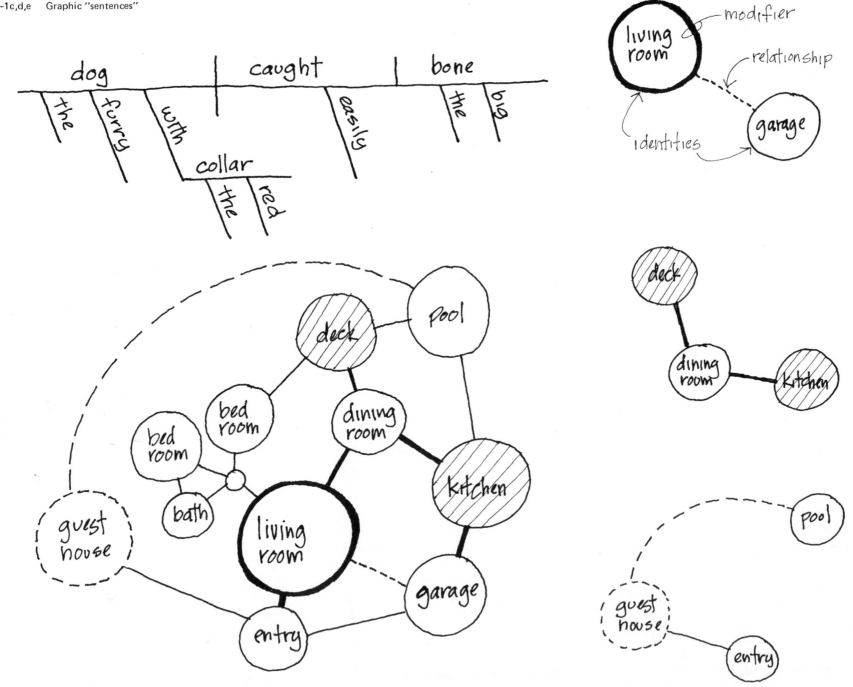

4–1a   Sentence diagram
4–1b   Graphic diagram
4–1c,d,e   Graphic "sentences"

4 Abstraction I: A Graphic Language

"The design process can be thought of as a series of transformations going from uncertainty towards information. The successive stages of the process are usually registered by some kind of graphic model. In the final stages of the design process, designers use highly formalized graphic languages such as those provided by descriptive geometry. But this type of representation is hardly suitable for the first stages, when designers use quick sketches and diagrams . . . It has been accepted for years that because of the high level of abstraction of the ideas which are handled at the beginning of the design process, they must be expressed necessarily by means of a rather ambiguous, loose graphic language—a private language which no one can properly understand except the designer himself. . . . the high level of abstraction of the information which is handled must not prevent us from using a clearly defined graphic language. Such a language would register the information exactly at the level of abstraction it has, and it would facilitate communication and cooperation among designers."[1]

My own version of a graphic language is based on experience with students in the design studio and research in design process communications. It is presented here because I am convinced that a "clearly defined graphic language" is important to design thinking as well as communication between designers.

"A language consists of a set of rules by which symbols can be related to represent larger meanings."[2] The difference between verbal and graphic languages is both in the symbols used and in the ways in which the symbols are related. The symbols for verbal languages are largely restricted to words whereas graphic languages include images, signs, numbers, and words. Much more significant, verbal language is sequential, it has a beginning, a middle and an end. Graphic language is simultaneous, all symbols and their relationships are considered at the same time. The simultaneity and complex interrelationship of reality accounts for the special strength of graphic language in addressing complex problems.

The graphic language proposed here has grammatical rules comparable to those of verbal language. The diagram of the sentence (a) shows three basic parts: nouns, verbs, and modifiers such as adjectives, adverbs and phrases. Nouns represent identities, verbs establish relationships between nouns, and the modifiers qualify or quantify the identities or the relationships between identities. In the graphic diagram (b) identities are shown as circles, relationships are shown as lines and modifiers are shown by changes in the circles or lines (heavier lines indicating more important relationships; tones indicating differences in identities). In the sentence diagram, the verb shows a relationship that the subject has to the object, the dog caught the bone. The line in the graphic diagram is bi-directional; it says that the living room is connected to the kitchen and that the kitchen is connected to the living room. Thus the graphic diagram contains many sentences as:
(c) The very important living room has a minor relationship to the garage.
(d) The dining room must be connected to the special spaces, the kitchen and the deck.
(e) The future guest house will be related to the entry and indirectly to the pool.

GRAMMAR

There are other ways of drawing "graphic sentences;" three alternatives are shown here.

Position—an implied grid is used to establish relationships between identities; the resulting order sometimes makes the diagram easier to read (a).

Proximity—the degree or intensity of the relationships of identities is indicated by the relative distances between them (b). A significant increase in distance can imply that no relationship exists. This type of diagram has more flexibility than the former type.

Similarity—identities are grouped by common characteristics such as color or shape (c).

These alternatives may also be combined to form other grammatical variations (d) but care should be taken to retain consistency. In order to communicate clearly, the grammatical rules should be immediately evident. "The binding fact of mental life in child and adult alike is that there is a limited capacity for processing information—our span, as it is called, can comprise six or seven unrelated items simultaneously. Go beyond that and there is overload, confusion, forgetting."[3] One

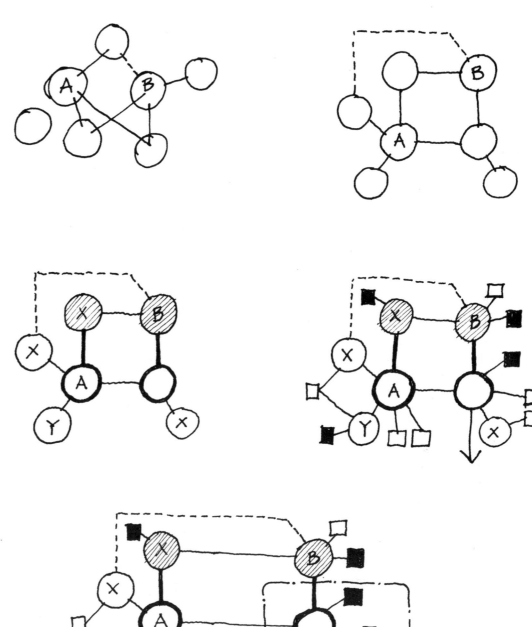

of the purposes for adopting some basic grammatical rules in graphic diagrams is to avoid confusion by reducing the number of variables to be handled at one time.

One of the most useful qualities of graphic communication is that information can be transmitted and received on several levels, simultaneously. Artists recognized this long ago. Successful paintings usually appeal to the viewer as overall compositions, renderings of detail, and technique with media, just to name a few of the levels. These levels of communication can be used to good advantage in a graphic diagram. The basic process for building a diagram (4-3) is:

1. Try to illustrate the basic identities and their relationships in a rough diagram.
2. Reduce the diagram to its simplest structure by applying rules of graphic grammar.
3. Modify the diagram to indicate a second level of information, using tones or heavy lines.
4. Add other levels of information as tag-ons to the basic diagram.
5. If the diagram becomes too complicated break it into segments by grouping or placing a boundary around identities.

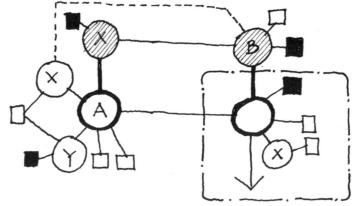

VOCABULARY:

Identities

There are a great number of ways of symbolizing an identity. The more common symbols are represented here in horizontal rows. The identity of these different possible groups is achieved by contrast. Usually all variables are held constant except for one. The number in each group is limited because most of us are unable to deal with more than five or six variations in one graphic diagram. The elementary symbols can be supplemented or replaced by numbers, letters or other symbols. By judiciously combining different groups of symbols it is possible to have several levels of information in a graphic diagram without sacrificing clarity.

Sometimes identities are best shown with a more tentative quality using dotted and irregular lines. Later chapters will further explain this less definite need.

Relationships

As with identities, different relationships are best represented by sets of line types. These line types can also be used as borders for grouping identities as a means of segmenting a diagram or of showing special relationships.

The arrow is a very special device for indicating relationships. As a symbol of movement, it has compelling qualities: ". . . any movement in the environment automatically attracts attention because movement means change of conditions, which may call for a reaction."[4] Arrows combined with lines can indicate a one-way relationship, a sequence of events, or a process. Separate arrows can be used to mark important parts of a diagram or to show dependencies and the feed-in of supplementary information.

Modifiers

Identities and relationships are modified according to an hierarchal system. In this manner, the significance of parts and the different levels of intensity in the relationship between parts are expressed. Hierarchy can be shown by different line widths, multiple lines, or the relative size of dashes and spaces in dashed lines (a). Graded tones and the accumulation of parts are also useful devices (b).

Modifiers can also create emphasis, principally through contrast in terms of size, tone, contour, or detail. Emphasis signals a special identity or relationship, segregates interwoven diagrams, or indicates special points or steps in a process (c).

Other Graphic Vocabulary

Several disciplines have developed their own shorthand symbols to facilitate rapid communication. Many of these symbols have a wide enough understanding to be useful in graphic thinking. Some of the most useful symbols, taken from the disciplines of mathematics, systems analysis, engineering and cartography are shown on the following pages.

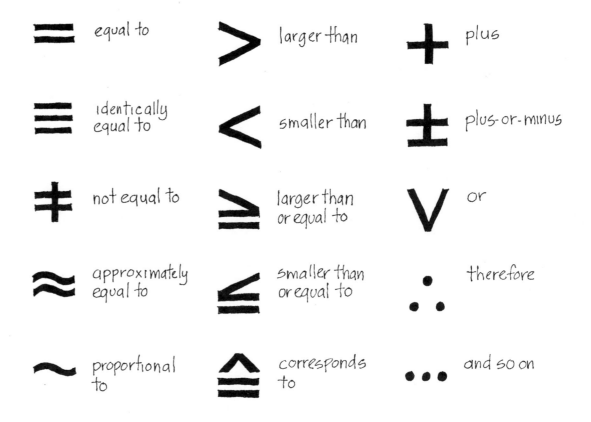

= equal to

≡ identically equal to

≠ not equal to

≈ approximately equal to

~ proportional to

> larger than

< smaller than

≥ larger than or equal to

≤ smaller than or equal to

≙ corresponds to

+ plus

± plus-or-minus

∨ or

∴ therefore

... and so on

Operations research and the analysis of communication systems led to the study of processes which, in turn, led to many applications of process management. With the study of more complicated processes, a diagrammatic language was developed in order to properly describe these processes (a). On the basis of a few symbols and a set of rules for using them, very elaborate processes can be readily explained in graphic terms. Some of the symbols shown to the right are useful in describing architecturally-related processes such as project plans, construction organization, and programmatic functions (b).

On the facing page are several symbols used in electrical, mechanical, and transportation engineering which can further extend our graphic vocabulary.

Basic Elements

The beginning and end of a sequence.

Decision: Yes or No

Miscellaneous forms:

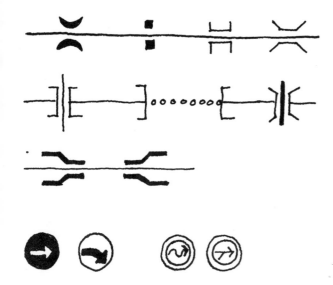

THE USES OF GRAPHIC LANGUAGE

"Unless detail is placed into a structured pattern, it is rapidly forgotton. . . . Detailed material is conserved in memory by use of simplified ways of representing it."[5] The graphic 'vocabulary' just presented was selected because the symbols are commonly accepted, simplified ways of representation. Since our graphic vocabulary will continue to expand graphic communication, we must use symbols commonly understood and a clear grammatical structure as a context for the vocabulary to be effective. The obvious corollary is our necessity to become graphically 'literate.' We need to become familiar with a range of graphic languages. "The thinker who has a broad command of graphic language not only can find more complete expression for his thinking but can also recenter his thinking by moving from one graphic language to another . . . in effect he uses language to expand the range of his thinking."[6] This last point is extremely important to a full use of the material presented in this book. Communication and thinking are intertwined purposes; we need to focus on how they assist each other rather than ask which is more important.

Graphic language can have pitfalls as identified by Robert McKim.

1. Lack of skill or inappropriate choice of language can be damaging to tender new concepts.
2. Mistaking graphic images for reality
3. Glamorizing an idea
4. Concealing what should be revealed
5. Habitual use of a few languages avoids some types of mental operation.

1.

2.

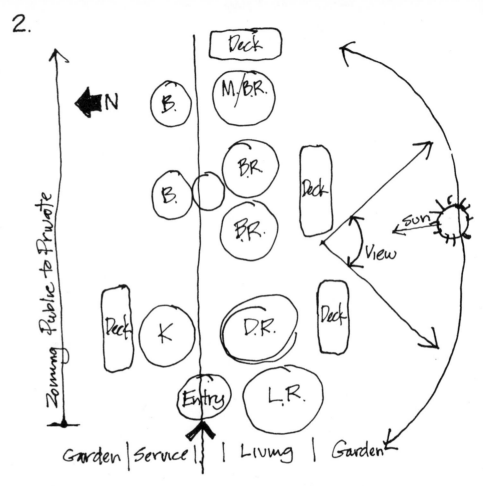

TRANSFORMATION FROM PROGRAM TO SCHEMATIC DESIGN

To close the discussion of graphic language, we return to the challenge of handling information "exactly at the level of abstraction it has" throughout the design process. In the example shown, the process is in stages of lesser abstraction from the building program to a schematic design for a house (the transformations after the schematic design which lead to the final building are preliminary design, design development, construction documents, and shop drawings. These are not shown because effective conventions already exist for

representation of those stages; there are several sources for examples of those drawings, including books and the drawing files of architectural firms).

The first diagram is an abstraction of the program of the house. The functions and the relationship between functions are indicated as well as the hierarchy of these functions and relationships. The major access points are clearly visible. The "bubbles" have no positional significance because the program does not contain that sort of information. If the relationship links between functions are

retained, the bubbles can be moved to several different positions without changing the basic information of the diagram, as in the smaller diagrams. The second diagram responds to site and climate information establishing both position and orientation of functions with respect to each other and the site. Natural light and heat, views, building access, and zoning of functions are also considered. The third diagram reflects decisions on scale and shape of the spaces required to accommodate the programmed functions. Here, consideration is given to functional needs and a planning grid. In the fourth diagram, specific structural,

Most Private

Private

Semi Public

Public

Quiet Garden

Working Garden

Open Garden

Outdoor Dining

Entry Porch ↑

construction, and enclosure decisions come into play. Sufficient formal definition has been indicated for the diagram to be called a schematic design.

This transformation from program to schematic design is only one of vast numbers of paths that could have been taken. By understanding the intent of the diagrams at each stage, we insure that options remain open, rather than lock into one form too early.

Most designers will agree that designing is not a "clean" process; in other words, it is not automatic, even-paced, directional, orderly or rational. We would probably agree that it is highly personal, discreet while holistic, sometimes very clear and sometimes quite obscure, sometimes rapid and sometimes painfully slow, exciting and also tedious. In short, it is very human rather than mechanistic. And that is why so many of us are so passionately hooked on designing.

Drawings, the visual language, designers use reflects all of the qualities I have attached to designing. In the following chapters I have tried to recognize the variability and individu-

ality of design processes by not associating graphic thinking with one design process. Rather I have presented the uses of drawings as discreet events; to uncover the breadth of richness that exists and leave open to each of us all of the ways and styles of graphic thinking or designing that we prefer, that we enjoy!

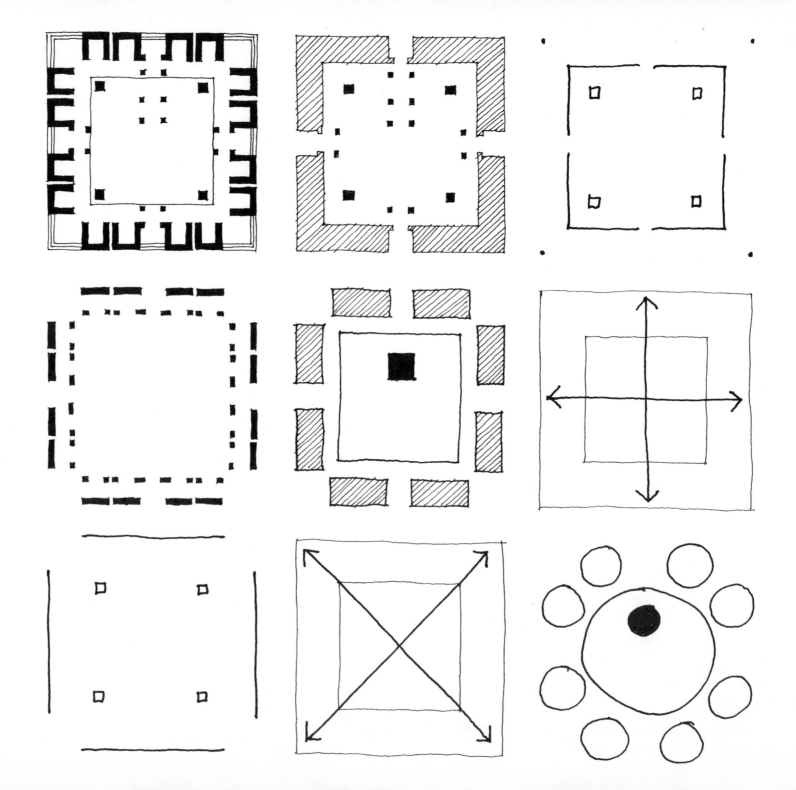

64

5 Abstraction II: Design

5-1   Abstractions of Hurva Synagogue project,
       Louis Kahn, Architect

5-2   Volkswagen drive assembly

"Practical design problems are variable and idiosyncratic. They generate a variety so great that it is nearly impossible to describe such problems let alone understand them. Despite this, practicing designers must interpret these problems if they are going to deal with them."[1] Architects must simplify problems, reduce them to their essential elements. This is the process of abstraction, the exposure of underlying structure or pattern of a whole system. As we will see, graphic communication is well suited to the task of abstraction. The simultaneous view of the abstract sketches keeps the whole structure of a system up front.

A discussion of a system and its analysis is helpful to understand the functions of abstract sketches. Design problems are generally caused by the poor functioning or breakdown of a system. If I can't get my car started on a winter morning, I know the cause could be a frozen gas line, a malfunctioning starter, worn-out spark plugs, the distributor, the battery, or even an empty gas tank. A car is a system of parts, all of which must interact properly in order for the engine to start. The system extends beyond the car parts to include routine maintenance, the manufacturer's inspection of parts, keeping moisture out of gas station storage tanks, and my checking the gas gauge

regularly. In order to solve the problem with the car that does not start, we must understand it as an organized system. If the distributor is not the cause of the problem, no degree of inspection of the distributor could solve the problem. In design, this understanding of the whole system is referred to as holistic analysis. ". . . the whole *must* be subdivided if we are to analyze it . . . If we choose the wrong kind of subdivision, then the whole will be destroyed, whereas other kinds of subdivision may throw its structure into relief. Angyal considers four ways of subdividing a whole, such as a plant, an animal or some inanimate

object. One could cut it at random, thus producing a collection of unrelated parts; one could divide it, according to some preconceived and fixed principle that failed to take its inherent structure into account, which would represent a rational approach; one could abstract distinguishable properties from it, such as size, shape, color, consistency and so on, which would represent an empirical approach; or one could divide the whole *according to its structural articulation*."[2] Abstract sketches can express the structural articulation of a system. Here are some ways, still using the automobile as an example.

5-3a Abstraction by distillation
5-3b by reduction
5-3c by extraction
5-3d by comparison

Engine

transmission

1. Distillation—Removing from the drawing all those things which are not important to the analysis of the structure of the system's critical parts: highlighting the electrical system.
2. Reduction—Representing groups of parts with a smaller set of symbols makes it easier for most of us to understand the drawing and entertain changes; there can be several levels of reduction yielding increasing generalization. This diagram represents only the major automobile systems (electrical, mechanical, fuel, etc.).

3. Extraction—Through contrast or emphasis a part can be given special attention while remaining within the context of its system: position of the distributor in the electrical system is stressed.
4. Comparison—Casting different systems in the same graphic language facilitates comparison of structural rather than superficial characteristics of different systems.

In design or problem solving, products, processes, beliefs or other systems need to be represented in several ways ranging from con-

crete to the most abstract. ". . . operations often require imagery that is abstract and pattern-like. Which is not to say that abstract imagery is more important than concrete; rather, abstract and concrete imagery are complimentary. The flexible visual thinker moves readily back and forth between the two."[3]
"A way to obtain literacy and at the same time to acquire language flexibility, is to learn how to use graphic language to move thinking and expression from abstract to concrete meanings and back."[4]

5-4a   Structure of design problems

5-4b   Misfit between need and context

5-4c   Misfit between need and form

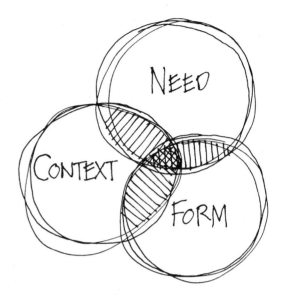

ABSTRACTION APPLIED TO ARCHITECTURAL DESIGN

The application of the tools of graphic abstraction to architectural design is aided by an understanding of the structure of architectural design problems. Horst Rittel has identified three variables of the typical design problem: "(a) *Performance variables* which express desired characteristics of the object under design, and in terms of which the object will be evaluated ("construction cost," "aesthetic appeal," "overall quality," and the like). (b) *Design variables,* which describes the possibilities of the designer, his ranges of choice, his design variables ("height of ceiling," "shape of door knob," "type of heating," and the like). (c) *Context variables,* which are those factors affecting the object to be designed but not controlled by the designer ("land price," "likelihood of earthquakes," "type of eating habits," and so forth.")[5]

A problem can be said to exist when there is some sort of misfit among these three variables in an environment. The design problem is solved when, as indicated in the diagram, there is a satisfactory relationship between *need, context* and *form.* Consider a small printing

company as an example. The original *need* was to accommodate a printing operation in the *context* of the downtown of a small city and the *form* provided was a small, one-story building. Over time, new problems occur due to different types of misfits:

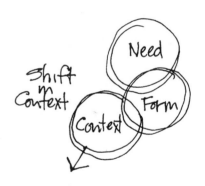

1. need/context—property values and the tax rate increase rapidly even though the building still meets the printer's needs.
2. need/form—the operation outgrows the building or the building deteriorates and is not adequate for the need.
3. form/context—a change in the zoning restrictions makes a one-story building no longer a sound financial investment.

The design problem can be caused by a change in any one or a combination of the variables. The solution to the problem may lie in the change of any one of the variables or a combination. The design solution is not synonymous with the designed building rather, the design drawings are the embodiment of a new balance between need, context and form. The success of the design solution is measured by the way it responds to all three variables. The categories of need, context, and form can also provide a convenient structure for organizing

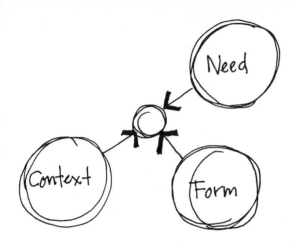

design project information. Design concerns, issues, priorities, or, as shown here, criteria can be gathered under these variable headings. This promotes a balanced view of the design problem and a more complete evaluation of design alternatives. (The application of evaluation criteria will be discussed further in the chapter titled Verification.) In this section, we will deal with the graphic abstraction of the architect's design problem as described by *need, context,* and *form.*

Need:
Space Requirements
Relationships
Priorities
Processes
Objectives
Maintenance
Access
Equipment
Environment

Context:
Site
Zoning
Services
Macro Climate
Micro Climate
Adjacent Buildings
Geological Factors
Vehicular Access

Form:
Zoning
Circulation
Structure
Enclosure
Construction type
Construction Process
Energy
Climate Control
Image

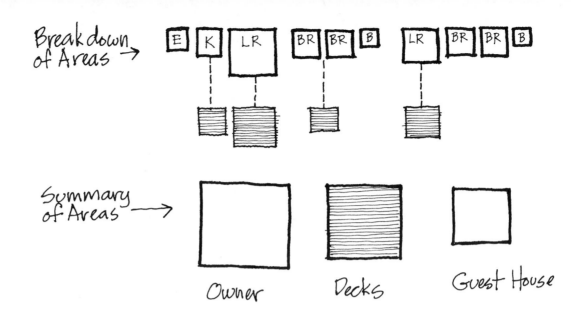

Need

The building program or brief usually contains most of the information about the client's needs. Programs for the average-size project, such as an educational or institutional building, can be quite complex. Although the program for our example, a four-bedroom recreational residence, is not very complex, it should serve to illustrate the basic types of diagrams that could be used to describe functional needs.

The first step is to get a good grasp of the quantifiable aspects of the program. Using squares to show the area requirements for different functions, the relationships of size are quickly apparent (a). A summary of basic program areas (b) helps consider some of the basic zoning alternatives and relationship to usable site area. Another quantitative diagram that can be quite useful (c) shows intensity of activity or use. The intensity of functions is shown by the relative sizes of the circles, and the volume of circulation between functions by the width of the connecting bars. Detailed estimates of the intensity of activity are not usually made, but direct observation and informal analysis based on the designer's past experience should be sufficient to make the diagram useful.

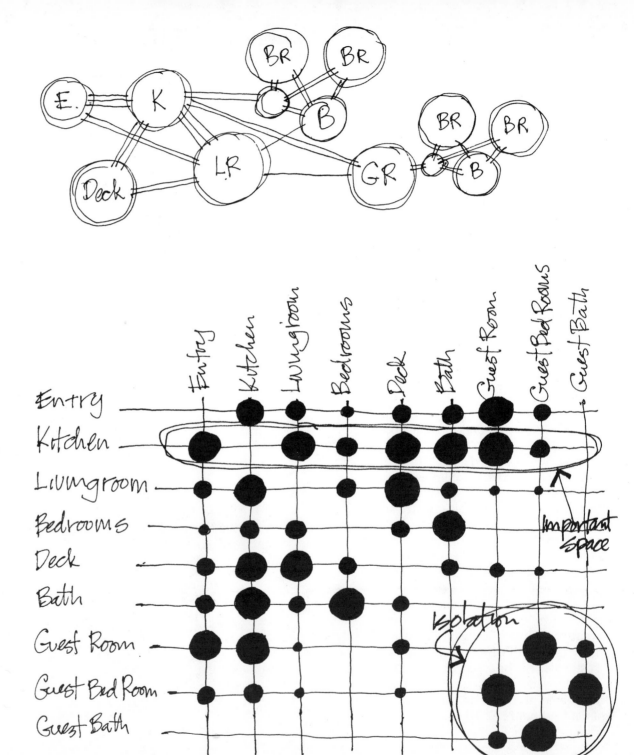

Relationships

The "bubble" diagram has become a familiar tool to architectural designers. It can abstract the building program to conveniently summarize the activities to be housed and their required relationships.

As we saw in the last chapter, bubble diagrams are also easy to manipulate as the designer moves from building program to building design. As long as the basic rules of the graphic language are followed, these diagrams permit wide flexibility of thinking.

Another type of relationship diagram is the matrix. All the functions are listed along two perpendicular axes and then the relationship of each function to the other functions is categorized. The advantage of such a matrix is in the ways it can be read by the designer. This example demonstrates that the kitchen is a critical point of relationship for the whole family and their guests; that the sleeping areas should be isolated from each other and from most of the rest of the house; and that the access to the guest areas should be controlled. While it is true that most of these observations might be made intuitively for a house, the matrix promotes a restructuring of thinking that can stimulate new insights regarding needs such as separation or communication particularly in more complex buildings. Finally the matrix provides a simple graphic reinforcement of the designer's memory as he considers the building context and form.

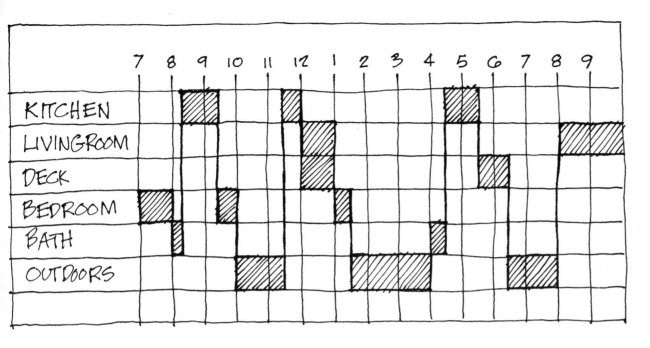

Physical Behavior

While we might assume that most people use houses in pretty much the same way (judging from new housing development design), there are differences. These differences can have a lot to do with the comfort of a family in a particular house. One way of illustrating the use of a house is to make a log of spaces occupied by different family members during a typical day. The results may be surprising, and encourage the client to look at housing in a new way. There may also be implications for design priorities, orientation of spaces, and energy management.

Circulation is one of the under-considered functions inherent in a building program. Many of the experiences of a house, its impact on people, take place as they move through and between spaces. These are referred to as kinesthetic experiences; they are dynamic experiences unlike sitting or standing in one space. Some architects have suggested that scenarios of desired kinesthetic experiences, in a graphic form, can be very useful to design. In its simple form, a kinesthetic map may use symbols for different experiences, but it is also possible to key perspective sketches to the map and help create a sense of what is desired. Again, such diagrams help the client and the designer discuss and think about the design problem.

5–12a Matrix diagram of relationships between design issues and spaces

5–12b Revised matrix indicating priorities

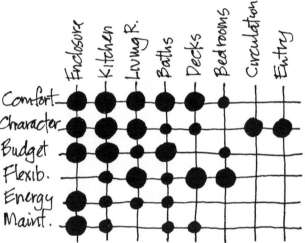

Design Priorities

To make a successful house, an architect must help the client choose his priorities as his desires often exceed what is financially possible. But priorities remain a vague notion for most people until they see a specific building design with a price tag. Then comes the pruning and pushing and pulling, ending with a design that looks like it has been through a street fight.

A matrix diagram clarifies priorities so the client can better understand them before pro-

ceeding to building-form alternatives. The matrix starts with a list of design issues and a list of functions. At each point of relationship in the matrix, we ask what is the importance of this issue to this function. The degree of importance is indicated by the size of the dot. When this process has been completed for each issue, the most important issues and functions (those with the highest accumulative degrees of importance) can be identified and a hierarchical list of issues and functions formed. When the matrix is reconstructed with issues and spaces arranged in their order of

importance, it is possible to make some observations about critical areas of the design problem.

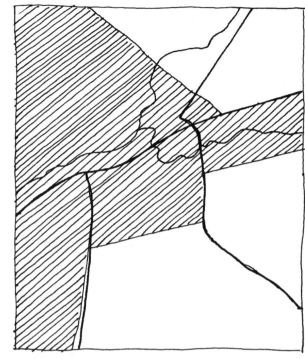

Context

The identification of context variables helps the designer to set problem boundaries and places constraints on the number of design options available. The experienced architect welcomes these constraints because they help to focus his attention on the really viable alternatives. Context variables include: site, climate, zoning or building ordinances, finances, time, and available construction technologies.

Site Selection

A composite graphic display of the effects of different criteria on site selection can assist both client and designer in choosing a site. The mapping starts by grouping several criteria under a few basic headings such as land availability (which might include the considerations of cost, opportunity, or services), geological characteristics, and zoning. Maps are made for each basic heading, showing the land which meets the criteria. The maps can then be overlayed to form one composite map. Now the most favorable sites can be easily identified and second choice sites will also be evident.

SITE

TOPOGRAPHY

Site Analysis

Site features can include macro and micro climates, topography, natural circulation, views and landscaping elements such as trees, bushes, rocks, or water. These site features must be considered in order to place and design a house. Abstract sketches can uncover problems and opportunities by showing the site features simultaneously. The illustration used here focuses on general site characteristics rather than on specific details. Focusing on generalities helps the designer to form a visual memory of the important site considerations. With the aid of these sketches, other perceptions can be derived such as wind, privacy buffers, or the best site for building. For this recreational house the sun pattern, the ridge in the land and the summer breeze suggest the general orientation of the building. The existing site entry, disposition of the trees and the small river to the south set up the prominent views and basic site circulation. This site analysis can be further extended taking into account program area needs to explore some preliminary alternatives for building massing, as shown at the far right.

PRIVACY

WINTER WIND

VIEW

SUMMER WIND

WINTER
SUMMER

N

CLIMATE

Buffer zone for privacy and quiet.

Buildable zone

ZONING & VIEWS

SINGLE STORY

TWO STORY

COMBINATION

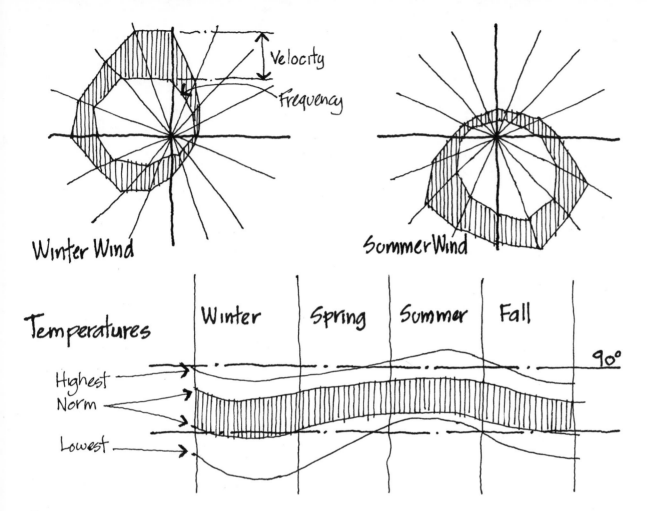

Winter Wind

Velocity

Frequency

Summer Wind

Temperatures

Winter   Spring   Summer   Fall

90°

Highest
Norm
Lowest

Precipitation

Days of Sun.

Rain Days

Snow Days

Other useful abstract sketches can present a more refined view of the action of climate over time. With energy conservation becoming a major consideration in housing design, we need more dynamic models of the action of climatic forces such as wind and sun. It is becoming easier to obtain reasonably accurate statistical data on weather, but the graphic presentation of this data is what makes it usable to the average designer.

Linked Boxes

Grouped Boxes

Opposing Boxes

One-Way Grid

Continuous Wall

Buffer Wall

Extended Walls

Two-Way Grid

Form

The third set of variables, form, is under the control of the designer. In this area he can help the client make decisions after the need and context variables have been identified. But remember: the solution to the design problem is basically an agreement between need, context, and form. In a sense, all three sets of variables are flexible until a fit is achieved. Some designers expect the client's program and the context alone to dictate the solution, but form is equally important since there are a number of viable forms that meet specific needs. The architect must be as familiar with form variables as with those of need or context. The abstract sketches which follow are used to build a visual memory of form variables.

Space/Order

Variations of the spatial organization of a house are numerous. A few examples are shown here in plan diagrams using a similar drawing style to facilitate an easy comparison. The walls are drawn with heavy lines so the diagrams can emphasize space by clearly defining solid and void. Furthermore, titles are given to each organizational type as an important aid for easy recall.

On the following page, a range of organizational types show three dimensional options for spatial order and the implications for appearance. Structure and materials are also indicated.

Horizontal Plane over a Platform

Double Plane

Cage

Open Box

Closed Box

Solid Wall & Canopy

Solid Wall & Skylight

Parallel Load-bearing Walls

Chiseled Block

5-20 Alternative enclosure types

Human Scale

Hierarchy of Scales

Proportion Analysis

5-21   Important human-related sizes

5-22   Dormitory building, New York University,
        I. M. Pei and Associates, Architects

5-23   Entrance facade, villa at Garche, LeCorbusier

Scale/Proportion

Although the qualities of form can be enjoyed by everyone, architects do not automatically perceive how the form variables are arranged to achieve a specific effect. In addition to their formal education most architects spend a lifetime learning about them.

One effective way of increasing perception is through visual analysis. The emphasis of a specific variable such as scale or rhythm in a sketch can be abstracted out of the context of the building. Scale implies a relationship of

sizes. The size of people is the most handy reference for other sizes; this is called *human scale.* Though it is obvious that all structures can not be within our scale, we can feel more comfortable with a large building if certain of its features range in size from human scale to the overall building. Through graphic analysis, we can begin to understand how scale is handled in different buildings.

The effect of proportions on the design of a building can be represented for analysis in a similar way. Proportion is the relationship between dimensions (horizontal-vertical).

Through abstraction, the impact of proportions on existing buildings can be better understood.

Weight & Permanence

Lightness & Flexibility

5-24a   Traditional brick construction
5-24b   Curtain–wall construction
5-24c   White Residence, Mitchell/Giurgola Architects
5-24d   Grabbeplatz at Dusseldorf, James Stirling, architect

5-25a   Evenly–spaced windows
5-25b   Casa Mila, Antonio Gaudi, architect
5-25c   Wolfsberg Center, Alvar Aalto, architect
5-25d   Boston City Hall

Balance in asymmetrical facade composition

3D composition

Mass/Balance

Anyone who has taken up jogging is well aware of the importance of mass and balance in human experience. We all have a built-in sense of these qualities causing us to respond to them in buildings. Further, mass and balance are associated with many other feelings such as security and flexibility. In a building, a sense of mass can convey security or permanence; a sense of airiness can convey flexibility or freedom. Throughout architectural history, many methods have been discovered for varying the apparent mass of buildings. By analyzing buildings which have clear sensations of mass, the use of formal devices as horizontality, verticality and emphasis can be uncovered (a).

Walking is a tremendous feat of balance. Much of the enjoyment of walking, riding a bike, skiing, and the like is derived from the tension between stability and instability. We have a finely-tuned sense of balance which carries over into our visual perception. The different ways of articulating balance in building design can be also highlighted through abstract sketches. The sketches shown here (b) deal with symmetrical and asymmetrical balance in composition and three-dimensional balance, an important part of architecture.

Repetition / Staccato Rhythms

Legato Rhythm

Accelerating Rhythm

Multiple Rhythms

Repetition/Rhythm

One way of achieving unity in a building is through repetition of parts which are alike such as windows or columns. Similarity of objects even if only partial similarity, is a way of emphasizing association. Members of the human race are recognized by a number of similar features in spite of the great diversity in appearance of individuals.

The importance of rhythm in architecture is based upon its relationship to the human rhythms, walking or breathing, and natural rhythms, the tide or the seasons. Just as music presents audio rhythms, architecture displays visual rhythms. In architecture the principle means of achieving rhythm is spacing of parts; this is comparable to the intervals between beats or notes. The character of visual rhythms in a building depend on the size of both the intervals and the parts. Two basic types of rhythm can be identified. Staccato rhythm is formed by clear distinction between intervals and parts such as mullions on a curtain-wall. Legato rhythm is softer, formed by more subtle transitions between intervals and parts as in the curvilinear architecture of Gaudi. There are also rhythms distinguishable by patterns of interval or part sizes, as in a facade by Palladio. And there are accelerating or decelerating rhythms as in the Wolfsberg Center by Aalto.

5-26a   South facade, Litchfield High School Gymnasium, Marcel Breuer and O'Connor & Kilham, architects

5-26b   Ohio Town Hall project, Venturi and Rauch

5-26c   Assembly Building at Chandigarh, LeCorbusier

Unity/Diversity

The degree of unity or diversity expressed in a building constitutes another class of form variables. The other variables, (scale, proportion, mass, balance, repetition, or rhythm), can be used to achieve unity or diversity. Some of the ways of increasing unity include: framing or emphasizing a border (a), continuous pattern (b), modular grid (c), use of a single shape which is at the same scale as the building (d), independence between the parts and the whole (e).

Diversity can be achieved by planned violation of the rules of unity: avoiding framing or consistent pattern, variation of rhythms or modules, multiple grids, breaking-up dominating geometry.

Unity and diversity are not mutually exclusive; it is possible to overlay them, and thereby increase the intensity of both attributes.

Too Complex

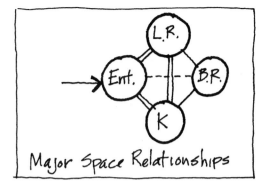

Major Space Relationships

Balance

ABSTRACTION AND PROBLEM-SOLVING

The ultimate use of abstract diagrams is to help the designer to commit to memory large amounts of project information. These diagrams can also be used directly as a record of design variables. The main advantage of diagrams as a graphic record is their immediately accessible information when all the diagrams are arranged in a large group. Creative designers fill sheets upon sheets of paper with diagrams and sketches of all types to record what they know and their thoughts on a design problem.

An abstract diagram must be simple and clear to be effective. If it contains more information than can be absorbed at a quick glance, it looses its effectiveness. Yet, it must provide enough information to form a distinct idea. Limiting the size of the diagram to a portion of our visual field is a method of partially controlling the amount of information given. A standard 8 1/2 by 11 sheet of paper fits within the visual field of a single individual, and the drawn diagrams can be as small as a half dollar. When several designers work as a group, the visual field is expanded considerably. The firm of Caudill Rowlett Scott has

Too abstract

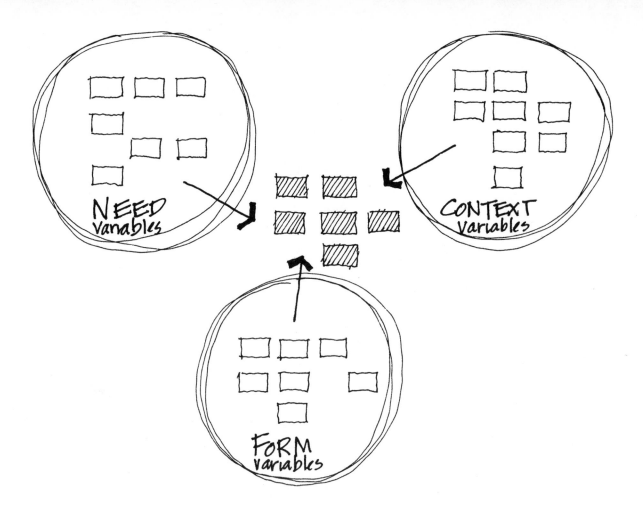

developed the "Analysis Card" technique for group work.[6] Diagrams, about the size of a hand are drawn on 5 1/2 by 8 1/4 cards (I have personally tried 3 by 5 and 5 by 8 cards with success). During the problem analysis and design process diagrams are drawn on the cards and these are tacked on the wall for display to the group. This results in a continual up-dated display of the group's thinking. As an added benefit, the cards are easily movable to provide flexibility of ideas by association.

For legibility, ink or felt-tip pens are preferable to pencil or other media. Line weights should be geared to the viewing situation: a fine-line pen is good for the individual but a heavier marker is better for group display.

SOURCES OF SOLUTIONS

As was pointed out before, the origin of a design solution may be found in any one of the three types of variables: need, context, or form. On the following pages are five studies based on the recreational house example. In each study, an abstract diagram of one of the variables is used as the source of a basic organizing idea for the house; then constraints or considerations from the other type variables are introduced to modify the concept. These studies should make clear some of the following advantages of abstract diagrams:

1. The variety of ideas visible at one time is very stimulating for thinking.
2. The differences in the three types of variables promotes a variety of solution alternatives.
3. Attention is focused on general issues instead of details.

CASE STUDY No. 1
response to site —

Need for a focal point

Second view

Principal Views

Guests   Main House

Bi-Nodal scheme

wind

Guests   sleep   Living area

Entry   deck

A

focal point
Possible entrance

view

views

Progression
to water

wind

B   Guests   House

B

Separate zones
&
Sense of progression

Section BB

Guests   Living

Utility   deck

Section AA

Compact scheme
with wind shield

CASE STUDY No. 2.
enclosure vs exposure

Privacy & wind protection

Sun & views

Problem with North entry!

Kitchen & utility

Guest & Sleep.

living

deck

sleeping above

Kitchen/utility

Stair

Guest

Living

Hall

Deck

CASE STUDY No. 3
activity analysis

Entry

BR.

BR

B.

K

L.R.

Deck

2nd Entry from Recreation & Guest House

Barrier

K   LR

Move kitchen

Service Core

R

LR   Deck   B.Rs.

Protected

E.   K.   B

L.R.   B.R.   B.R.

Deck   Outdoor dining

winter wind

Stacking

Guests

Family

CASE STUDY No.4
Topography / Light / Air

Freestanding

Platform

Cantilevered

Cut & Fill

Site adaptations

Summer

South Porch

North Light

Reflected Light

Breezeway

Venturi Effect

Rise of Hot air

Summer

Winter

CASE STUDY No. 5.
Enclosure / Planning Grid

Proportion Control

Closed Box

MBR | B | BR | BR | B | GBR

LR.

K | Deck | Deck

sleeping | Living | deck

Box with skylights

Bi-nodal Box

guests

trapping heat in Winter

89

6 Manipulation

Manipulation is defined as "skillful handling or operation; artful management or control."[1] The purpose of manipulation in graphic thinking is the altering of graphic images so as to get a new look at them and thereby expand our thinking. While the architectural design process involves decision-making aimed at the reduction of alternatives in search of a final solution, it also involves elaboration aimed at expanding the range of possibilities. Most architects are not content with solving problems with existing knowledge; they want to expand the knowledge base at the same time. Architects are opportunity-seekers as well as problem-solvers. The drawings in this chapter are devoted to elaboration in the design process, deviation from the norm, expansion of thinking, and development of imagination.

We are just beginning to understand the untapped potential of our imaginations. Intuition, creativity and imagination have traditionally been considered the skills attributable to a limited group of people: inventors, artists, geniuses. Many researchers of creativity feel that most people have the basic capacity for imagination but that it remains underdeveloped or unused. "It is simple enough to list those 'attributes of creativity' which are needed by the designer and to point out the reasons for their inclusion. But actual development and refinement of such behavioral characteristics is difficult since society makes it a relentless battle, an often thankless and rarely positively reinforced chore, to maintain such behavior. The same society which readily accepts the creative 'product' will chastise or deny the creative 'activity' required for such production because of its non-typical nature."[2]

Making creative behavior acceptable is the first step in promoting creativity in architectural design and this chapter tries to provide more information about creative thinking with sketches to support it. If we can get through some of the mystery surrounding the personal approaches taken by architects, I believe specific techniques can be identified which make up a body of trainable skills.

We will be looking at three approaches to manipulation:

1. Open-ended images that suggest a number of different perceptions or interpretations.
2. Transformation of images.
3. Structuring or ordering images.

ELABORATION
opportunity-seeking

REDUCTION
decision-making

Design Process

These approaches are aimed at recentering visual thinking. "Recentering vision is fundamentally an experience in unlearning. For most people, breaking lazy, category-hardened, fear-inducing habits of seeing is an educational task of considerable magnitude."[3] To make full use of these drawings for graphic thinking we must be comfortable with exploration that is not tightly focused, let the mind wander, and be open to unexpected results.

OPEN-ENDED IMAGES

Terms like ambiguous, collage and multivalent have been used to describe works of art and architecture which can be "read", interpreted, or appreciated simultaneously on several levels. These works are often said to have several meanings. Design sketches often have similar qualities of ambiguity allowing the designer to think flexibly and in general terms. I refer to this as open-ended. Open-endedness can be achieved with transparency. This approach is based on the tradition of showing depth location by overlapping Modern art introduced mutual overlapping producing a transparent effect that allows two or more figures to occupy the same place. In concept, developing a transparency allows the designer to suspend decisions about the exact location of spaces or the boundaries

Overlapping

single interpretation

Transparency

double interpretation

Suggestion

6-5 By LeCorbusier. Strasbourg project

6–6   By Louis Kahn. Concept study, University of
       Virginia Chemistry Building

6–7   By Gerald Exline

between spaces. Another approach to open-endedness is the incomplete, obscure sketch. By providing minimum information, the sketches focus on the most general issues while establishing the essential character of the architecture. The tentative feeling of the lines help give some sketches an added sense of being temporary. To achieve a similar effect, some designers use a soft pencil to produce a wide fuzzy line.

Open-ended sketches often convey a sense of immediacy and the confidence of the designer. Notice how few lines provide an impact. The white spaces help to pull the eye back to the key parts of the drawing. To produce effective sketches, the designer is required to work quickly and in a relaxed manner; the sketches should not become an end in themselves but an enjoyable process.

TRANSFORMATIONS

The purpose of open-ended images is to *invite* changes in the images. Transformations, however, are *specific* changes made in the graphic images. The possibilities for change in graphic images are practically unlimited, but we will look at just a few basic types of transformation. They are topological continuity, ornamental grammar, reversals, and distortion.

Graphic transformations can be very helpful to creativity in design. The stages of creativity have been described as "Preparation, Incubation, Illumination, and Verification. . . . the period of incubation frees the individual from previous fixations, . . . he is then able to see the problem with new eyes when he returns to it."[4] Transformations are aimed at changing perspective or perception, making the familiar seem strange. It is important to remember that a period of preparation must precede incubation. The designer prepares by becoming immersed in the problem, trying to understand all the variables of need, context, and form. Once the problem becomes imbedded in his mind, he attempts to overcome preconceptions about the possible solutions by changing the existing graphic images.

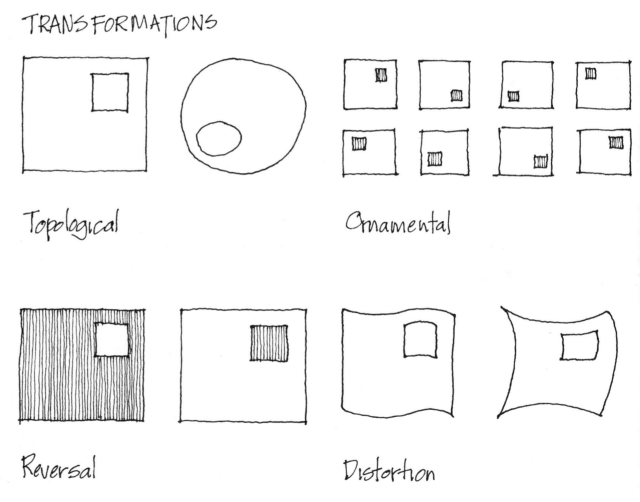

TRANSFORMATIONS

Topological

Ornamental

Reversal

Distortion

6-9a   Topological similarity between a donut and a cup

6-9b   Evolution of topologically equivalent house plans

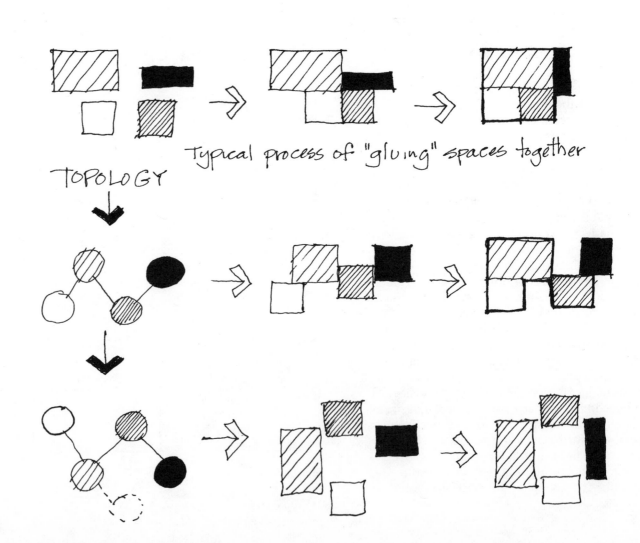

Typical process of "gluing" spaces together

TOPOLOGY

Life House 1938   Sundt House 1941   Jester House 1938

Topographical Similarities

Topological Continuity

In mathematics, the term topology is defined as "the study of those properties of geometric figures that remain unchanged even when under distortion, so long as no surfaces are torn."[5] A practical example of two objects topologically similar but different in appearance is the donut and the cup. The transformation from donut to cup shows how the same basic surface relationships are retained while the form is pushed and pulled.

A similar topological continuity is important to the manipulation of design images. Many architectural students mistake a specific arrangement of parts for a topological or essential relationship of parts. If the true topological characteristics of a diagram are identified, many other arrangements of the parts can be explored.

March and Steadman pointed out the potential of topological continuity in comparing three houses by Frank Lloyd Wright. "In them he uses a range of 'grammars,' by which he meant, above all, the controlling geometric unit which ordered the plan and pervaded the details. . . . Whilst they may look different, they are in fact topologically equivalent. If each functional space is mapped on to a point and if, when two spaces interconnect, a line is drawn between their representative points . . . we find that they (the houses) are topologically equivalent in plan, . . ."[6] Therefore one topological structure was open to three very different expressions.

1. TRANSLATION

1. Ornament from tomb at Gourna, Thebes. Owen Jones, Pl. VII, no. 4.

2. ROTATION

2. Ornamental Mosaic pattern at Pompeii. Owen Jones, Pl. XXV.

4. Ornament from a Greek vase. Owen Jones, Pl. XVI, no. 15.

3. Ornament from tomb at Gourna, Thebes. Owen Jones, Pl. VIII, no. 16.

4. INVERSION

3. REFLECTION

5. Translation and Reflective Inversion

5. String course over the Panathenaic Frieze, Parthenon, Athens. Owen Jones, Pl. XXII, no. 18.

6. Slipped Reflection, or Alternation

6. Band ornament from Greek vase. Owen Jones, Pl. XVII, no. 58.

7. Acceleration

7. Ornament from Egyptian mummy case. Owen Jones, Pl. VIII, no. 17.

8. Deceleration

8. Ornament from Egyptian mummy case. Owen Jones, Pl. VIII, no. 12.

9. Figure—Ground

9. Plaited straw from the Sandwich Islands. Owen Jones, p. 15.

6-11 By Thomas Beeby. Basic manipulations of ornament

6-12 By Thomas Beeby. Applications of ornamental grammar

Ornamental Grammar

Thomas Beeby, in his article, *The Grammar of Ornament/Ornament as Grammar* clearly illustrates the application of ornamental grammar to building massing and design at many scales by the master architects of the modern movement. Specifically in the work of Le Corbusier, he shows the impact of the traditional training in ornamentation principles. A direct means of achieving a rich complexity in building forms is revealed. "Le Corbusier's early training in ornament placed a valuable method of working within his grasp. The principles found in Owen Jones and transmitted to Le Corbusier through L'Eplattenier remained with him throughout his career."[7]

Beeby describes "four basic manipulations of a unit to create ornament: translation, rotation, reflection, and inversion. The simplest type of band ornament, translation (illustration 1), is the repetition of the unit, always in the same orientation, along a horizontal axis.

Reflection   Reflective Inversion   Slipped Reflective Inversion   Rotation

Unit   Inversion   Reflective Inversion   Rotation

Le Corbusier, plan for the Carpenter Center, Harvard University, Cambridge, Massachusetts, 1961–64. (Diagrams by author, plan after Le Corbusier.)

Rotation (illustration 2) is the repetition of the unit around the point of intersection of two adjacent sides. It accounts for pinwheels and other spiral configurations. With translation and rotation, the unit merely slides along the surface of the plane, in a straight line or a circle, but in both reflection and inversion the unit is flipped over in space to present its under side. With reflection (illustration 3), the unit is flipped over on one of its edges, producing bilateral, or mirror, symmetry. With inversion (illustration 4), the unit is flipped over its central horizontal axis. More complex configurations are derived from a combination of these four basic operations. Translation accompanied by reflection is probably the most familiar. Translation accompanied by reflective inversion is another typical operation (illustration 5). The complexity increases through devices such as shifts along the horizontal axis, or glide line, leaving gaps between units, to produce slipped reflection, or alternation (illustration 6). . . . Also, by accelerating (illustration 7) or decelerating (illustration 8), the rhythm through decreasing or increasing either the size of the units or the distance between them, one can transform scale."[8]

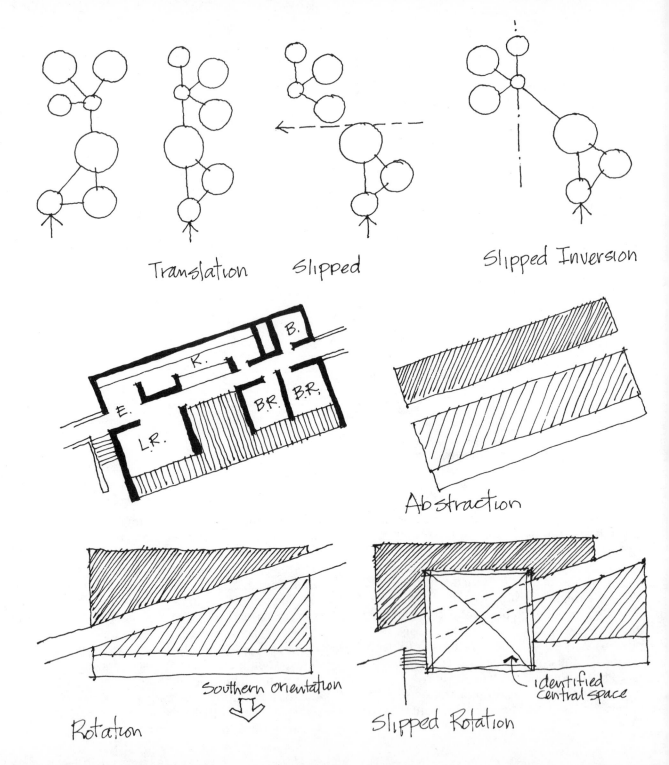

Translation   Slipped   Slipped Inversion

Abstraction

Rotation

Southern orientation

Slipped Rotation

identified central space

The implications of ornamental grammar for building design and planning are significant, but there are additional implications for the design process. Ornamental grammar can be used to transform more abstract graphic images, routinely uncovering new thinking. For example we could take a program bubble diagram and through its rotation, reflection or inversion change the starting point in problem-solving (a). Another approach would start with a schematic plan; from this, an analysis drawing would be made to reduce the concept to basics, and the abstract drawing would be run through some ornamental transformations to uncover alternative concepts or insights into the structure of the original design (b).

Taoist symbol

Group   Individual

chaos →
Yin & Yang

Oranges   ↙ blue/grey cloth

Reversals

Reversals are focal changes from what was first considered to be its complement. Their usefulness derives from the qualities of its contrasting complement. The Chinese philosopher, Lao Tse, held that the essence of everything we can see lies in what we cannot see; the essence of man is not in his physical appearance and the essence of architecture is not in the visible structure. The Taoist symbol Yin and Yang represents the absence of order, chaos, as a black background; the two revolving forms are Yin and Yang, the contrasting complements which make up order, night and day, a musical note and a pause, active and passive. The ideal condition, perfection, is symbolized as a dynamic balance between opposites: groups of people are defined by individuals and individuals are defined by groups; the color of an orange changes in intensity with the changing background. Architectural examples of complements are walls and openings, materials and the joints between materials, vertical and horizontal, rectilinear and curvilinear. To change our perceptions, we change the emphasis of an image to its complement or contrast.

Wall

Openings

Material

Joints

The simplest form of reversal is called figure-
ground drawing. Two sketches are made of
a subject such as the Piazza of San Marco.
In one sketch, the buildings are shown in
solid black and in the other sketch, the space
between the buildings is shown in black.
By looking at the two sketches at the same
time, it is possible to get a better understanding of both space and buildings, and the
relationship between them. Figure-ground
sketches can be used to study elevations of
buildings, patterns, profiles, massing and
many other problems.

Reims

Ronchamp

Predominant Orientation of Beach House

Exposure

Enclosure

Water/Beach

Open View

Controlled View (evokes imagination)

Attempt to hide Column in a wall

Exposed Column

6–16   Reversals of architectural experience

Another type of reversal is experience reversal. If the normal kinesthetic experience of a church progresses from small to large scaled spaces, a reversal of scale can evolve a new form. If it is normal for a beach-front house to be open and be oriented to the view, introduce enclosure and inward orientation. The Japanese tea house uses the wall to deny views in order to intensify the view seen through a small window. Designers sometimes have a problem trying to hide a building element when the solution would be to emphasize that very element.

a.

b.

c. BONANZA BANK

tellers?

loans

Vault

officers

special services

o Tellers don't usually work this way. What would happen if they worked as a team? Would customer feel he is getting more service?

o Perhaps a more relaxed, accessible atmosphere would be helpful.

Graphic images can also be used to reverse thinking processes. Instead of thinking of spaces as bubbles glued together, consider them as carved out of a solid block (a). If a circulation sequence has been seen as a series of spaces, concentrate instead, on the passages (b). When a student gets hung-up on one design solution or finds trouble developing an idea, I suggest that the given building program be forced into a typical facility for a highly contrasting program or activity as in banking in a restaurant, a hospital function in a country club setting, a home in a factory.

6–17a   Reversal of perception, positive vs. negative space

6–17b   Links vs. nodes

6–17c   Restaurant vs. bank

6-18a   After M. C. Escher lithograph, *Balcony*, 1945

6-18b, c   analysis of lithograph

6-19a, b   Distortion of a bubble diagram

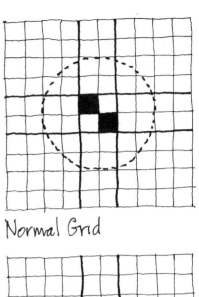

Normal Grid

Distortion

Distortion

The Dutch artist, M. C. Escher, created a wonderful world of fantasy through optical illusions based on the representational systems of the Renaissance. He achieved distortions which dramatically alter our view of reality through simple manipulation of these representational systems as in the lithograph, *the Balcony*. By way of a reversal of the projection method used for maps of the world, he imposes a simple grid over the conventional drawing and then doubles the size of the central section; thus the distorted grid is used as a reference system to complete the drawing.

The grid-manipulation method can be used as a simple way of distorting other types of drawings. For our purpose, the grids should be kept quite simple to remain in a sketch style. The examples of the bubble diagram on this page and the building plan on the following page show just a few of the possibilities for grid distortion. Simple magnification or reduction of the scale of an image can produce a distorted effect. In addition, there are a number of special projection techniques such as 360 degree views which are potential tools for distortion sketches.

Normal Grid

Distortion

STRUCTURING OR ORDERING IMAGES

Peter Carl made an important observation about the "plan libre" developed by LeCorbusier, represented here by the plan for the villa at Carthage. "The importance of this invention is two-fold: the use of gridded and layered space as a contextual device, and the nature of subsequent spatial gestures on those terms."[9] This is the basis for another method of transformation of images, namely, the use of ordering devices to create an artificial context within which new responses can be made.

Of course, generation of space and form by the use of geometrical patterns is not a new approach. In the eighteenth century, K. I. Dietzenhofer used a pattern of interlocking ovals to develop his Baroque church plan. Frank Lloyd Wright used rectilinear, triangular, and circular grids as the basis for house designs. More recently Walter Netsch designed buildings based on two square grids rotated to a 45 degree relationship, and Portoghesi and Vigliotti have developed houses within circular fields.[10]

Villa at Carthage

Baroque Planning Grid

Wright / Hex-grid

Planning "Field

Circular Grid

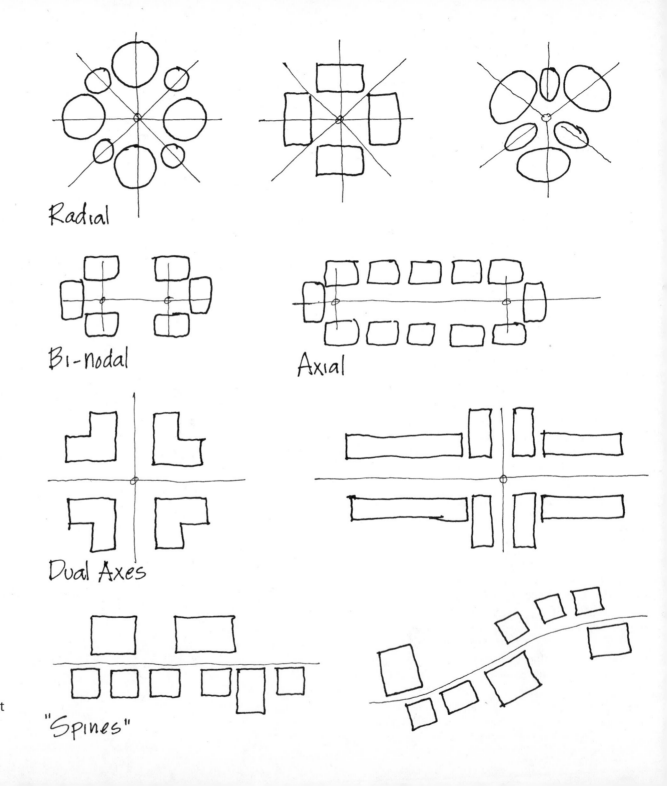

Radial

Bi-nodal

Axial

Dual Axes

"Spines"

Points and lines can be used in images for ordering functions or spaces, transforming the information into a new form. Points provide a focus for radial compositions of a wide variety. When two points are placed in close proximity, binodal configurations can be developed; but as the two points are pulled further apart, a line is formed, opening up a number of axial arrangements. Axial orders include: dual axes, major with minor axis, and parallel axes. Lines can also be used as "spines" for collecting and organizing a number of different spaces; these lines, referred to as datums, can be either straight or curvilinear.

On the facing page the basic orders of point and line are extended or combined to form several ordering devices of varying degrees of complexity. They are not included as a kit of devices as much as they are meant to suggest possible manipulation alternatives by which each designer may evolve his own tools.

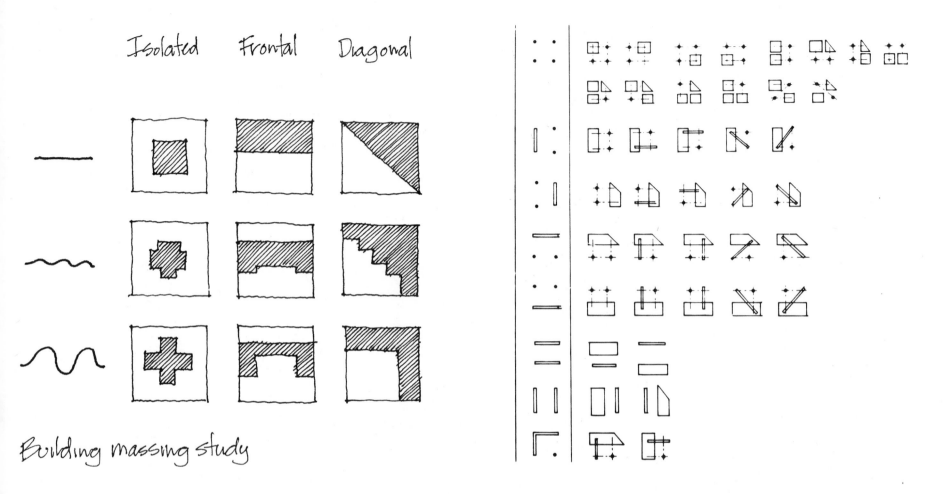

Isolated   Frontal   Diagonal

Building massing study

6-28   Matrix diagram of building massing alternatives

6-29   By Thomas P. Truax. Matrix of alternative
groupings of an urban complex

The matrix provides still another way of applying order to the transformation of images. The first example illustrates the basic application of a matrix. Different concepts of building placement on the site are shown across the top and different degrees of articulation are indicated in the vertical direction. By showing the combinations of the two considerations, a number of forms evolve. The second example (from a student project) is a search for alternative configurations of an urban zone development. The basic orders are shown in the left vertical column and different combinations of city blocks, in the right column. From these, different interpretations are formed.

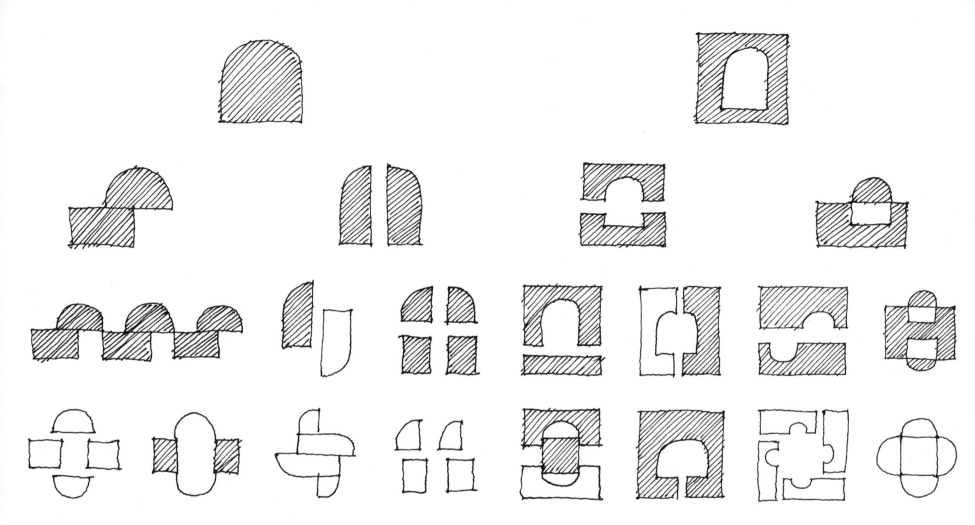

A PYRAMID OF POSSIBILITIES

It is my hope that, as you begin to experiment with some of the sketch techniques in this chapter, the loosening-up and freedom from rigid thinking will open up an exciting new perspective about designing. It can be an energizing experience that becomes addictive. Relax and enjoy it!

Part of the potential of manipulation derives from the fact that ideas breed ideas. As the graphic thinking cycle gets moving with ease, the group of ideas rapidly expands in a very rough pyramidal progression. If only two new images are perceived for each one drawn, the growth in ideas can be amazing; but for many designers this is a big 'if.' They are afraid of "wasting time" by following their instincts or indulging in the fantasies of free association. Designers, also, have difficulty in suspending judgment of ideas; they censor them before they ever get them on paper. And so they never get a chance to have a new look at their ideas, detached from themselves. The situation is comparable to an aspiring song writer who never has his music played for other people. In isolation, he may be able to develop his music to a point, but without testing it through the responses of other people, he will be handicapped.

6-31   By Alvar Aalto

If we look closely at the notes and sketches of some architects, the rapid growth of ideas becomes obvious. The growth is sporadic and multi-directional. Attention shifts from the scale of a plan or site plan to details of windows or handrails. There are also shifts in the types of sketches. Some architects rely heavily on plans as vehicles for concept development, others work exclusively in elevations, while still others are most comfortable with perspective sketches.

6-32 By Thomas Beeby

In this short chapter, we have looked at the use of manipulation in sketches as an aid to the processes of design incubation and creativity; but we have touched only on a portion of the material available which concerns the promotion of creativity. For a list of particularly good sources on this subject, check the bibliography in the back of the book under creativity. Below, a helpful list of manipulative verbs from *Design Yourself* by Hanks, Belliston, and Edwards[12] might stimulate some ideas of your own.

MANIPULATIVE VERBS

Multiply	Divide	Eliminate
Subdue	Invert	Separate
Transpose	Unify	Search
Delay	Distort	Rotate
Flatten	Squeeze	Complement
Submerge	Freeze	Soften
Weigh	Destroy	Concentrate
Fluff-up	By-pass	Add
Subtract	Lighten	Repeat
Thicken	Stretch	Adapt
Relate	Extrude	Repel
Protect	Segregate	Integrate
Symbolize	Abstract	Dissect

7 Discovery

Most architects will recognize discovery or invention as an important focus of their work. It is the satisfying "payoff" that beckons the creative mind. The intensity of concentration in thinking is very exciting. Look at the sketch by David Stieglitz on the facing page. It immediately shows us the energy, the action, the joy of discovery. It also reveals the skill and confidence with which the architect attacks his project.

The success of discovery in design is greatly dependent on the quality and quantity of the other types of graphic thinking. Discovery can be compared to picking and arranging a bouquet of flowers, which requires a sense of design and practice. Graphic *representation, abstraction, manipulation, verification,* or *stimulation* are comparable to the preparation of the garden, the planting and tending of the flowers, without which there would be no bouquet. Discovery brings the power of the different types of graphic thinking to bear on a problem at a moment in time.

Before getting into the graphics that express discovery, I would like to digress for a moment

and discuss creativity in the profession of architecture. The field of architecture is commonly viewed as being creative and certainly some of the most creative individuals are architects. I believe that an architectural education is still one of the best curriculums for training creativity, although not a guarantee. Helen Rowan's report on studies of creative people identifies qualities which they all seem to share. These include: "a general openness to experience from both without and within; a toleration for ambiguity, confusion and disorder; the strong disposition to be independent rather than conforming; and

the tendency to perceive through intuition . . . focuses upon possibilities . . ."[1] Anyone who is or has been an architectural student will recognize these qualities; they permeate the traditions of architectural training from the wide variety of project types to crits and juries, to strong conflicts of opinion, having to defend one's ideas, to being asked to go further than just solving the problem.

Still, there is a question in practice about the overall impact of creativity on the design process. Out of expediency or lack of support from clients or colleagues, we may neglect the development of our creative abilities. We can and should foster creativity in architecture for the sake of ourselves as well as the profession. As Helen Rowan put it, ". . . the experience of this century suggests that the quality of individual life, and perhaps the survival of human life as a whole, depends on the ability and disposition of human beings to think original thoughts, to reshuffle familiar facts into new patterns of meaning, to perceive reality behind illusion, and to engage in daring leaps of the imagination."[2]

Hammer

Pole

Rock

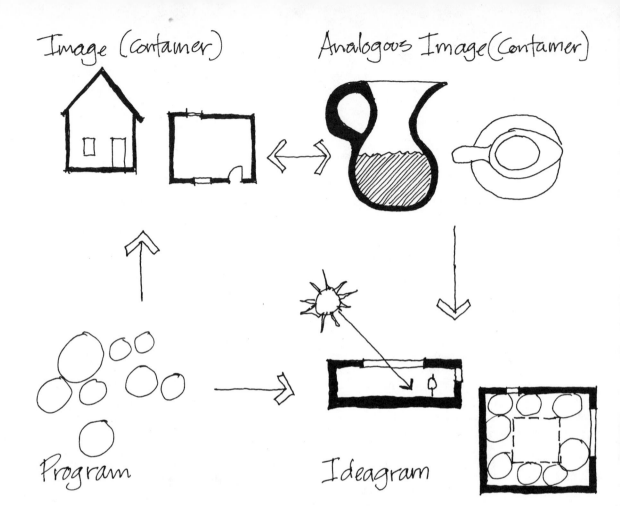

Image (Container)

Analogous Image (Container)

Program

Ideagram

THE DISCOVERY PROCESS

For the architect or the designer, the process of discovery consists of two parts: invention and concept formation. Invention seeks the basic discovery, the original idea for the project; concept formation converts the discovery into a graphic and verbal statement which can give basic direction to the full development of the project.

Invention

David Pye wrote that invention "can only be done deliberately, if the inventor can discern similarities between the particular result which he is envisaging and some other actual result which he has seen and stored in his memory . . . An inventor's power to invent depends on his ability to see analogies between results and, secondarily, on his ability to see them between devices."[3] The analogies are easily recognized in our everyday inventions. If we lack a hammer to drive tent stakes into the ground, we gain an insight to the solution by seeing a tent pole section or a rock at arms length analogous to a hammer.

Again, using the example of the recreational house, we can sketch out a basic approach to invention in architecture. The starting point is the abstract diagram of the program for the house. This leads to a choice of one image of a house, namely a container that holds people. Almost simultaneous with the house image we have an analogous image, the pitcher, as a container of liquids. In the fourth sketch, the ideagram, the house program and the image of the pitcher are combined to form a specific discovery of how the recreational house might take shape. In this example, the house is also seen as a container of energy, admitting solar energy through a hole in the top similar to the hole in the top of the pitcher. The concept for the house could be formed from this ideagram or the analogy

7-3   Analogy between a hammer and a pole or rock

7-4   Analogy between a house and a pitcher of water

Top Entry

Cantilever

7-5a, b   Extensions of the pitcher analogy

7-6   By Leonardo da Vinci. Studies of a temporary structure for festivals

7-7   By LeCorbusier. Images for the Philips' Electronic Poem

could be extended further through observations such as: the only entry into the pitcher is through the top, so perhaps the major entry into the house could be via a stair dropping into the central court. Since the pitcher is supported as a cantilever from its handle when picked up, maybe the house could also be cantilevered from supports on one side.

The graphic thinking sketches which architects have used provide evidence for analogy-taking in their design process. Often these sketches are very small in order to pursue many different analogies on the same piece of paper.

This permits the designer to work loosely and entertain all sorts of ideas; original trains of thought are recorded and can be returned to at will. Combining images derived from sketches can also generate further variations.

117

Symbolic Analogies

Spreading hand

Foot prints

Direct Analogy

Evaporation Cooling

air

Shade

air

Water

Evaporation Cooling

Shade

air

air

Water/pumped to the roof.

Analogies

In his book *Synectics: The Development of Creative Capacity,* William Gordon described four types of analogy: symbolic, direct, personal, and fantasy.

The example of the pitcher and the house as containers is a *symbolic analogy,* a comparison between general qualities of the two objects. Other symbolic analogies might be made between the spread of a hand and the extensions of a house or between footprints and canopied pavilions which loosely constitute the house.

Direct analogy compares parallel facts or operations. In the above example, the house is designed to have the same cooling characteristics as a tree: shade, evaporation, and air movement.

In a *personal analogy,* the designer identifies himself directly with the elements of the problem. Assuming that the prime consideration for this house is warmth and comfort on winter days without large uses of non-renewable energy sources, the designer might imagine himself to be the house. To make himself comfortable, he might lay close to the

ground below the ridge so the cold wind can pass over his head. This can be translated into a low-profile, house below the ridge with trays of space covered by sloped glass skylights to admit the warm rays of the sun.

The fourth type, *fantasy analogy,* uses a description of an ideal condition, desired as a source for ideas. In the case of our recreational house, the designer might fantasize a house that opens itself up when the client arrives on the weekend and automatically closes up when the client leaves. It could be compared to a tulip that opens and closes with the action

Personal Analogy

Fantasy Analogy

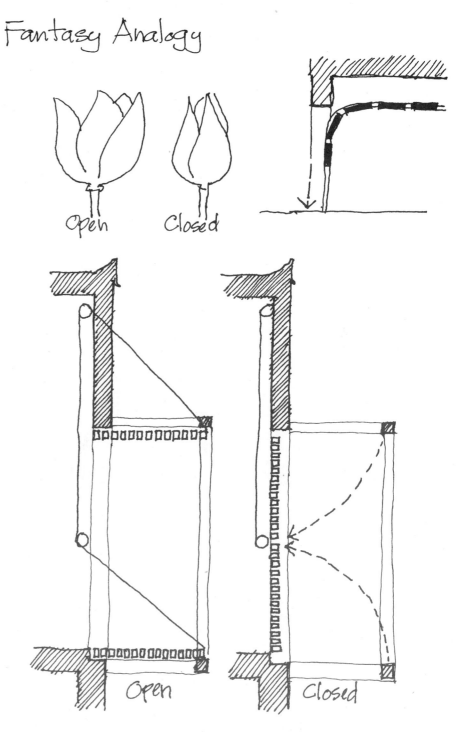

Open   Closed

Open   Closed

of sunlight, or the automatic garage door, or a puppet that comes alive when you pick up the strings. The decks and the roofs over the decks could be like the leaves of the tulip. But how do they open and close? A motor is another energy consumer; is there another way? How can the puppet strings help? The final solution uses ropes and pulleys to raise and lower the flaps. The system is balanced so that the weight of a person on the decks can pull up the roofs, and the dropping of the roofs could pull the decks back up. The decks and roofs would be held in both open and closed positions by spring latches.

PHYSICAL ANALOGIES

Structural

tap root

"Mile-High bldg"
tap root

Mechanical

slow down of a stream of water

slow down space in museum

Control

Flower opening in response to the sun

Louvers opened by photo cell in response to the sun.

ORGANIC ANALOGIES

Plant

differentiation within limits

shutters painted by tenants

Animal

task training

computer controlled house maintenance

CULTURAL ANALOGIES

Man

self awareness & actualization

Japanese tatami mat rooms change able for the occasion

Society

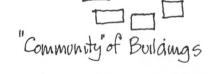

Community

"Community" of Buildings

Symbol

artistic language

Building language

Solar heat storage

Sources of Analogy

The possible models from which to draw analogies can be classified by categories as physical, organic, or cultural and the subcategories include:

1. Structural—referring to shape or relationship
2. Mechanical—the way something operates
3. Control—maintaining a condition
4. Plant—goal orientation and differentiation
5. Animal—behavior
6. Man—imagination and choice
7. Society—interaction, competition, organization
8. Symbolic—conventions, references, suggestion

Often architects or designers limit their thinking to structural or mechanical analogies. The samples of the range of analogy types, shown on the facing page, should suggest some alternatives.

Increasing Effectiveness

We have all experienced times when our mind appeared frozen; a single thought which doesn't seem good enough or unable to solve a critical problem. Here are a few specific approaches which might help thinking get moving again.

Eolithic Design: Sometimes designers succumb to what Robert McKim calls "functional fixedness," the "tendency to sort objects into indelibly labeled containers."[4] As a result, they are unable to see their problem in any other light; kitchens or bedrooms, for example, are seen as having a single use. One cure for this difficulty is eolithic, or "found object" design; the normal use of an object is disregarded in favor of a new use. Examples include barrels of water used for heat storage, trees used as sculpture inside a house, doors used as counters. The counter and storage setup of the kitchen could be used as a model for a studio or other work space, and the bedroom might be converted into a dining or lounging space. The "found object" approach can also be used with ideagrams; the binodal organization of a typical shopping center might be used in a house to generate more movement and interaction.

Escape: Sometimes just getting away from the problem is enough to loosen the mind and open fresh views of the project. Escape can

Tree as sculpture

Door/Table

Pillow in a box

Sound Amplification

take the form of diversions such as entertainment, or sports, or games; it can also be simply rest and relaxation, or "sleeping" on the problem.

Random Thoughts: Even when not actually working on a problem, our subconscious mind is often still trying to solve the problem. Then suddenly, we get an idea or an answer to the design problem. Some designers have these insights just as they are going to sleep or upon waking. It is important to write or sketch these ideas before they are lost. For this reason, many architects carry a small notebook with them or keep paper and pen handy near their bed or another place of relaxation.

Sense Awareness: Working in a predominantly visual media can sometimes lead to ignoring the other senses and may cut a designer off from a large number of sources for analogies. If we think of a house as being soft as a pillow in a box, it might lead to the use of curvilinear partitions; comparing a house to a musical instrument could result in a metal roof to catch the sound of the rain or some way to amplify the sound of a breeze.

If this discussion of the use of analogies seems too simplistic, remember that great architects of this century. Wright, LeCorbusier, Aalto used simple analogies as a source for many of their inventions. Geoffrey Broadbent comments: "Most architects—and artists—are extremely reluctant to admit the sources of their analogies. They think that such admissions would somehow diminish one's respect for their creativity; but far from it—they will merely confirm that they have brains and mental processes which every other human being possesses. Our respect for them, in fact, might increase if they admitted that, given the *same* mental processes, they are able to make better use of them."[5] Broadbent goes on to describe a number of analogies that LeCorbusier used in his work and observes that he spent "a lifetime building up a store of analogies (his years of sketching being particularly fruitful). The analogies had become fundamental to his experience, absorbed, compared, contrasted, combined, overlaid by later experience, and changed by new perceptions; but they were there to be called on, and faced with a difficult design problem, LeCorbusier could draw on them. We too have our stores of analogies, not perhaps as rich as LeCorbusier's, but valuable nevertheless, because they are personal. Yet we fail to draw on them. It never occurs to us; they do not seem relevant and instead of that, we content ourselves by drawing analogies with other people's work."[6]

Concept Formation

The "basic concept," sometimes referred to as the "parti" is an enduring mechanism used by architectural designers to establish the fundamental organization of a building and guide the entire process of design development. The parti, at its best, provides:

1. The first synthesis of the designer's response to the determinants of form (program, objectives, context, site, economy, etc.)
2. A boundary around the set of decisions which will be the focus of the designer's responsibility
3. A map for future design activities in the form of a hierarchy of values and responding forms
4. An image which arouses expectations and provides motivation for all persons involved in the design process. This is often done through the use of abstractions ("My building is a spine" or "Our building bridges this gap.").

The typical parti sketch, like the one on the left by a fifth-year thesis student shows both the determinants and the basic resolution of the form. In this example, the sketch of a floating research station in the Atlantic Ocean illustrates the vertical pontoons secured by cables, supporting a multi-level platform; the basic interaction with water, wind, and sun is also indicated.

Ideagram 1.

Design 1.

The Ideagram

The sketches which have already been described as flowing from analogies, "ideagrams," are the starting point for concept formation. Ideagrams are extensions of analysis diagrams that can be used as:

1. An aid to investigation and synthesis in the design process
2. A framework in the design thinking process that leads to the final design product
3. A literal model of the final product; in architecture this is referred to as *conceptual clarity* in the building
4. An explanation of a design concept after the building design has been completed.

In order to show some of the potentials of the ideagram for developing design concepts, I have drawn three stages of evolution of an ideagram in the first column to the right. For each stage, there is a schematic design for a building in the next column; across the top, a literal translation of the ideagram into a building form. This approach has a clear, and forceful impact on the user. The effect is simple and dramatic. Across the bottom, a building form is being derived from a more complex ideagram. The resulting building

Ideagram 2.

Design 2.

Ideagram 3.

Design 3.

124

7-16a Willitts House 1902
7-16b Cheney House 1904
7-16c Hardy House 1905

Open Site

Compact site

Small/Sloped Site

may lack the simplicity or initial impact of the first building but in turn it may offer more variety of experiences.

Approaches to Concepts

As with other design skills, concept formation need not be a mysterious process developed solely through trial and error. There is a lot to be learned from those architects highly skilled at molding concepts; and here again sketches can be an important aid. On the next few pages, the analytical sketches abstract concept-getting techniques from the work of architects.

The first examples are from the work of Frank Lloyd Wright. In the houses known as "the prairie style," he used a basic plan of interlocking spaces dominated by a central hearth with an elaborate, indirect route of entry. Although the basic organizational partii remained constant, Wright's careful response to the unique constraints of each site produced a wide variety of building forms. As designers of houses, we can try to use Wright's basic parti or develop our own prototype plan and manipulate it in response to specific site conditions.

125

7-17a   Prototype concepts developed by Alvar Aalto

7-17b   Some applications of the prototypes

7-18a   Four house concepts by LeCorbusier

7-18b, c, d   Applications of the concepts

The Box

Catepillar in a Box

Catepillar out of the Box

Butterfly

Butterfly & Box

Resting Butterfly

Overlapping Geometries

Application of a Prototype

In the course of his career Alvar Aalto Developed a number of archetypes for buildings noted by their incorporation of multiple grids or geometries. Some of these archetypes are shown here in abstract form. The titles are one way of simplifying and remembering the different partis. You can use your own method of categorization, but it does seem helpful to be able to attach a one- or two-word label. Many of Aalto's concepts seem derived from the acceptance of two contrasting contexts within one building, as in the combination of urban and rural settings in the town center at Saynatsalo.

One of these archetypes could provide a starting point for the design of the recreational house. Or we could follow Aalto's approach to developing partis by looking for the double context in our project and evolving our own multiple geometries. Beyond this, there are a number of other variations which should show up as more sketches are generated.

Additive

1. Maisons La Roche et Jeanneret

Box

2. Villa à Garches

Small - Car Dealership

Frame

3. Villa à Carthage

Subtractive

4. Villa Savoye

Library

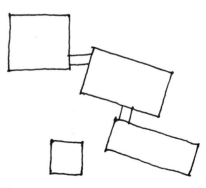

Museum

LeCorbusier was probably the most productive architectural inventor of the 20th century. His inventions have filled many books which I recommend you read. Roughly between 1922 and 1932, LeCorbusier designed four houses, each based on a different concept of a building. These were Maison La Roche (additive), Villa Savoye (subtractive), Villa Stein (closed cube), and the Villa at Carthage (open skeleton). When LeCorbusier illustrated and wrote about these four approaches to a building, he had built houses as examples. But this way of generating a building parti extends beyond housing in its potential utility.

Also shown on this page are applications of these partis to our sample house so you can see how to increase the number of concepts formed within the limits of a single project.

7-19 Matrix of twenty four alternative house
organizations based on concepts developed by
Moore, Allen and Lyndon

7-20 Three organizations of the recreational house
derived from the matrix

In their book, *A Place of Houses,* Moore,
Allen, and Lyndon explain six different ways
to organize rooms in a house and four different ways to incorporate machines (by which
they mean wet and service cores) into houses.
In the chart above, I have constructed a matrix
combining their two lists of alternatives to
produce twenty-four alternative prototypes.
There are a number of other "lists" that cate-
gorize ways of organizing buildings; these
could also be placed in a matrix to generate
additional alternatives. On the facing page
some of the prototypes are developed into
concepts for a house on our site, within the
constraints of the specific building program.

ORDER OF MACHINES / ORDER OF ROOMS	Rooms Around	Within Rooms	Outside Rooms	Between Rooms
Linked	1.1	1.2	1.3	1.4
Bunched	2.1	2.2	2.3	2.4
Around Core	3.1	3.2	3.3	3.4
Enfronting (exterior)	4.1	4.2	4.3	4.4
Great Room within	5.1	5.2	5.3	5.4
Great Room Encompassing	6.1	6.2	6.3	6.4

Kitchen

Bath (machine)

1.2 Linked Rooms
with machines inside.

5.4 Great Room With in,
machines between rooms

Large Dining/Kitchen

6.3 Great Room
Encompassing,
machines outside rooms.

Using table as a barrier in order to decrease personal distance

VS

Fold-up legs

Kitchen — a large comfortable space that promotes socializing
• hanging plants & natural light
◦ Easily accessible storage
◦ views of garden & children

Floor to ceiling cabinets

Family & Dining Room

Low Removable Dining table

Storage/Stereo

Piano

Patio-Garden

Garden Wall Scheme

garage below

Pattern Language

For several years now, a group at the University of California/Berkeley, headed by Christopher Alexander, has been working with a method of generating building designs, called "pattern language." Basically, it is an approach which constructs concepts for a building by combining prototypes for smaller parts of the building. The working tool is a hierarchy of prototypes: areas that combine to make rooms, that combine to make buildings, that combine to make communities, that combine to make urban complexes, and so on. Pattern language appears to be less a

prescription for the perfectly designed environment as it is a convenient format for formulating design concepts. Any designer is free to supply his own prototypes although there is certainly merit in sharing workable prototypes.

Application of the pattern language approach, on the simplest level, to our house project might take the following form:

1. Based on past experience, we would start with an array of prototypes for different spaces from which would be selected those that seem most appropriate for this

project. The prototype diagrams are quite simple with short verbal identifications for ease of identification and manipulation (a).
2. The diagrams are combined into a pattern which represents a summary of the building elements and shows an overall idea of the building (b).
3. The pattern is now manipulated to respond to the specific site context and special needs of the client (c).

At a more sophisticated level of application, as illustrated on the facing page, space prototypes or patterns are more specific and oriented

Livable Kitchen

Dining Space in a Townhouse Apartment

usually an interior room needing lots of artificial light and a sense of expanding space.

Solid or translucent canopy providing indirect lighting.

(3 x 5 card)

toward three-dimensional experience. The character of the space becomes a focal point for the identity of the prototype. The representational skills, discussed in an earlier chapter, are obviously of a great help here.

I have found two useful ways of collecting patterns and using them in design:
The building type notebook—An idea for a space is illustrated on an 8½ by 11 sheet of paper.These sheets are kept in a three-ring binder and used as a reference book for future projects.

Analysis cards—Patterns are recorded on small cards similar to the ones described in the second chapter on design abstraction. These can be filed by subject, ready to be pulled out for a specific design task. Whether using a card or a standard size sheet, it is helpful to use a common format. The basic information includes: a simple statement of the programmatic need and context ("dining space in a townhouse apartment"); a concise verbal and graphic statement of a prototypical response to the need; a more detailed description of the prototype or discussion of the pattern which is recorded on the back of the card or sheet.

When the designer is formulating concepts for the building design, he spreads the collection of relevant cards or sheets on a table or wall.

Patterns, or mini-concepts are then grouped as possible combinations and observed; but the designer must go beyond a simply additive process. "It is possible to put patterns together in such a way that many, many patterns overlap in the same physical space: the building is very dense; it has many meanings captured in a small space; and through this density, it becomes profound."[7] To achieve this sort of synthesis or "compression" of patterns, the graphic thinking process can be applied, using cards or a clipboard to turn over ideas as one scans the display of patterns.

CASE STUDIES

Examples of ideagrams developed into concepts for the recreational house case study are shown on the next two pages. The ideagrams, as you will recognize, are taken from the analyses of need, context and form in the chapter on abstraction, from the chapter on manipulation, and from this chapter. In forming the concepts, ideas which were derived from one source are reworked to respond to other concerns; prototypes, for example, are adjusted to fit this site or site-generated ideas are made to respond to the building program.

Bridge to study/retreat

overall Scape

closed up

Guests

Italian Village

Living Area

Pantry

Dock

Guests

Dining

LR

What about roots?

urbanizing the landscape

133

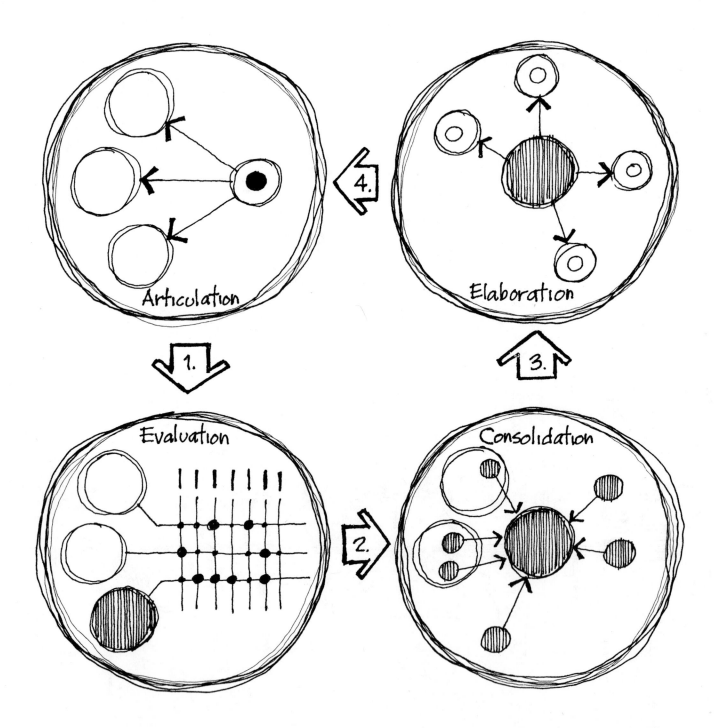

8 Verification

Within the realm of architectural design, verification refers to the usefulness of a design concept for a specific problem. The ultimate means of verifying the utility of a building design is a first-hand evaluation after the building has been constructed and occupied. However, post-occupancy evaluation would be of no help to the many decisions made in the process of designing and building. Therefore, architects usually go through a sort of pre-verification process. Within this context of pretesting design concepts, the utility of the verification mode of graphic thinking lies in moving from abstract images to more complete, concrete images of the design concept.

Verification can be described as a cyclical process producing images which are increasingly specific or concrete. For example, the image of a sheltering roof is converted into a low, long-span, hip roof, later having exposed wood trusses, and then to a specific color with wood shingles. The other progression of images is from larger to smaller parts of a building. One of the keys to quality design is the amount of attention given to the relationship of parts, from the building as a whole to the most detailed level. The Saarinens were said to believe that the success of any part of a building design lay in the study of the next smaller and next larger building element; design of a good room required the study of the furniture and of the building as a whole.

The model I use to explain the cyclical process of verification is shown on the facing page. There are four basic stages:

1. Articulation—The design image is extended through representational sketches of alternative expressions of the concept.
2. Evaluation—The alternative expressions of the design concept are tested against a set of criteria which represent a desirable performance. Evaluations of the alternatives are then compared.
3. Consolidation—The evaluation process usually generates a great amount of useful information in addition to the decision about alternatives. The purpose of consolidation is to try to incorporate as many good ideas as possible into the chosen scheme.
4. Elaboration—Having made a design decision at a new level of detail, the images now show the designer a whole new set of concerns from which he must form new design concepts. At this point, the recycling process is ready to start again with articulation of the new concepts.

Throughout the verification process, the choice of images must be deliberate, if the designer is to maintain control over design development. Simply put, you can't judge the performance of something you can't see. "If the concept is to provide any particular kind of spatial or kinesthetic experience, then the representative drawings must be eye-level perspectives. Concepts which are based on some desired relationship to the physical context must be represented in perspectives of that context if their success or failure is to be evaluated. Concepts which are based on particular relationships to the human figure might be best represented in sections which show those relationships. Any design solution is best studied and evaluated with those drawings which best show the success or failure of its conceptual basis."[1] And, therefore, it is necessary for the designer to have a wide range of sketching skills, from abstract to concrete, from loose to meticulous; and to understand the special potentials of the different images those skills produce.

Parti

Perspective

←—views
light
texture

8-2   A parti and three different forms of its articulation

8-3a   Three alternative expressions of the perspective
8-3b   Three alternative expressions of the plan
8-3c   Three alternative expressions of the section

1st Floor   2nd Floor

Plan

←—order
structure
module
zoning
proportion

ARTICULATION

In order to get a feel for the range of images that are used to articulate a concept, the three sketches shown on the right address some feature of the design concept. The qualities or characteristics illustrated are noted for each sketch. On the facing page, three alternative expressions are developed for each sketch.

A number of other implications of the design concept are articulated on the following page. They include such concerns as massing, scale, imagery, color, construction, flexibility, maintenance, territoriality, and comfort. While the experienced designer may not need to look at all these concerns within a given project, creative architects will often use a specific project context to reexamine accepted design norms.

Section

←—scale
proportion
light

1st Floor

2nd Floor

1st Floor

2nd Floor

1st Floor

2nd Floor

Flexible Zoning

square windows

Elevation Studies

Rethink base   South   East   North

Proportion analysis

Further Articulation

Interior Scale

Structural Organization

Kitchen Set-up

Dining

138

EVALUATION

The definition of evaluation, placing a value on something, implies that there exists a set of values to which the evaluator refers. When evaluating a design, we use "design criteria" to represent these values. The first concern of design criteria should be comprehensive, covering all aspects of the design problem. For the sake of convenience I have used as a model the design problem described earlier. Criteria are deliberately developed under each of the three categories of need, context, and form, and a checklist such as the one on the following page, is constructed to assure that we look at the design concept from every angle.

The second concern of design criteria is how and who's values they represent. When designing a building, decisions are usually made on the basis of competing sets of values held by the client, the designer, the intended user, and even society (in the form of customs or regulations). In addition to showing an array of criteria, a balance of values can be recognized by the weighting of the criteria. Differences in values will still have to be negotiated, but the designer can at least, illustrate the relationship between values and the evaluation of a specific design.

The third concern of design criteria relates to the differences in the way we look at design ideas. Some architects can be said to be more conceptually-oriented, that is, their evaluation is heavily influenced by such things as organization, consistency, and hierarchy as they are reflected in plans and axonometrics. Perceptually-oriented architects are more interested in the direct experience of a person outside or inside the building. In my opinion both conception and perception are important to the experience of a building and, therefore, important to the evaluation of design concepts. The designer must be aware of these two orientations of design and try to take a balanced approach to evaluation.

Conceptual

Perceptual

	NEED							CONTEXT					FORM				
	Communal space	Privacy	Orientation	Circulation	Energy conservation	Accomodation of functions		Views	Access to site	Building Privacy	Orientation		Hierarchy	Unity / Simplicity	Scale	Memorable image	Expression of functions
Alternative 1.	◉	◉	◉	•	•	•		◉		◉	◉		•	•	◉	•	•
Alternative 2.	•	•	•	•	•	◉		◉		◉	•			•	•	•	•
Alternative 3.	◉		◉	◉	•			◉		◉	•		◉	◉	◉	◉	•

◉ Superior
• Average
□ not adequately addressed

8-6 Evaluation matrix

A chart, such as the one above, is used to compare evaluations of the alternatives (see facing page). It lists design evaluation criteria under the headings of need, context, and form. For each heading, the criteria are listed in order of importance, starting from the left, therefore accounting for priorities. Alternatives 1, 2, and 3 are rated as providing a superior or average response to each criteria; blank areas indicate no specific response. This chart allows an overall view of the success of each alternative.

Making notes during the processes of evaluating and comparing of the alternatives is useful to further understand the strengths and weaknesses of these alternatives. In this manner, the designer can often identify the best ideas and expand on them with the information discovered through the display.

Good potential for spatial variety

Best balance of Communal space & privacy

remote studio

Could open up here

good Views

Simplest organization/ Strong hierarchy

Flexible space

⊠ Vs ⊟

B
BR
BR

E

ST

BR BR B

1st Floor

2nd Floor

fireplace location?

E

1st Floor

ST.

2nd Floor

North orientation for studio

E

1st Floor

Stair position disrupts axiality?

Strong orientation to the South

B

ST.

BR

BR

BR

2nd Floor

Views to outside

Sun entry in Winter

Good orientation for rooms

1.

2.

3.

141

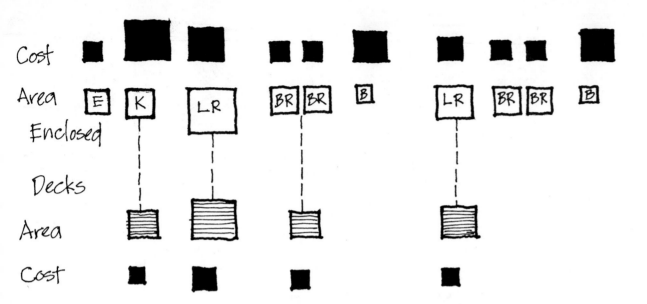

Cost-benefit

Some more examples of graphic images used to assist evaluation are on the next two pages. The diagrams shown above are an extension of analysis techniques developed by the architectural firm of Caudill Rowlett Scott;[2] the relative size of building areas and their approximate costs are shown side by side providing an overview of the relationship between program needs and costs useful to both client and designer.

Drawing Evaluation

Perspectives are so commonly used as "selling" tools that an examination of the perspective on the facing page might help to emphasize their potential as an evaluation tool. Here, the perspective is first rendered without conscious attention to the design of space. The drawing is now examined for clues of shortcomings. This approach is also applicable to finished drawings by professional renderers or even pictures of buildings by professional photographers.

Conceptual drawings can also be evaluated by reducing them to ideagrams which point up the clarity or consistency of the design concept.

Space more suitable for circulation?

Standing people may indicate difficulty of seating in central space.

bad joint!

fireplace is not strong enough form to dominate the space

Use of single floor surface points up complexity of space

off center stair still a problem

K | D.R. | D
LR. | I | LR
B | ST. | D

1st Floor

B | BR | BR
B | I
B | BR | BR

2nd Floor

alt.

Refine Fireplace central importance

Private Deck

B | BR | BR
st
B | BR | BR

Stair

Fireplace

8-11   Selecting useful ideas and combining them

CONSOLIDATION

Although the evaluation of alternatives helps us decide on the best route, a range of good ideas are uncovered which the designer will then attempt to incorporate in his final scheme. Many combinations are sketched as the design is pulled together and even at the stage of the completed design, some refinements are still incorporated. The designer seeks consistency in all parts of his design. The end result will be sketches that are more specific as to dimension, shape, and position.

Bath

B.R.s

open decks

Studio

Deck for Studio

Stone Retaining Wall

Covered North Entry

Attempt to nestle house in the ridge.

8-12   Resolution and refinement of the scheme

ELABORATION

With the basic design decisions made and clarified, preparation is underway for the next cycles of verification. Decisions at one level of design open up many problems at other levels. For example, fixing the design of a room makes it possible to study windows, flooring, mechanical systems, storage units, and a number of special items such as fireplace or solarium. Concepts for each of the parts are developed within the context of the design of the whole room. But each concept in turn can be verified by repeating the methods described in this chapter.

Entry Details

steel angles

slate

wood flooring

Built-in Bench Detail

Details

At some point in designing, the architect must assure himself that the design concepts are realistic by asking: can the parts be constructed? will they fit together? Detail sketches place the design under a sort of "microscope." The sample sketches on the next two pages show, through the different views, the importance of how something is put together and how it should look. Besides the up-close drawings, sketches must show the context for the detail.

Typical Fenestration Details

Interior Trim

wood hang Knobs

wood door Pull

Concept

Cliché

VERIFICATION AND EXPERIENCE

One of the advantages of experience in design is the opportunity to verify design concepts when the building is constructed. The designer has a mental store of the concepts he has verified first-hand; he knows what works and what doesn't. In addition, with a certain amount of confidence, he can generalize the new concepts from what he has learned and judged. As a result, many decisions can be made more quickly, facilitating the design process.

However, an ability to judge can sometimes deteriorate to the level of habit; and decisions are made before looking at the design problem. The repeated use of specific concepts, technologies or materials may lead to inappropriate preconceptions for the given problem. Many creative architects regularly retest accepted design concepts; they are constantly looking at their ideas, testing them, and evolving new concepts.

9 Stimulation

9-2   By David Stieglitz. Buffalo Waterfront
Redevelopment Project

The designer who wishes to take advantage of this second level of communication (being his style and the first level, the content of the drawing) should become aware of the range of qualities that can be communicated and useful techniques for doing so. The sketches in this chapter are offered as examples of what can be discovered. Each sketch conveys more than one quality, but I have tried to group the sketches according to one significant quality they each show.

This chapter concentrates on some of the attitudes and priorities architects and designers convey by the *way* they draw. It seems obvious that you can tell something about a designer through his drawings. Care in drawing often indicates care in thinking. In my experience, clients, consultants, contractors and others with which an architect works, are greatly influenced by his drawings; they set the tone for the work. The drawings are a way of telling people what you demand of yourself and a clue to what you expect of them.

IDENTITY

The drawings on these first two pages are significant for their strong sense of identity, a presence that says they are important and we ought to take time to look at them more closely. How does the *way* the sketches were drawn account for this quality? Both the style and the high constrast are important, but the fluidity of the sketches tells us about the intensity and confidence of the architect. We can almost see or feel the architect's hand moving over paper.

9-3   By Edwin F. Harris, Jr. Assisi

9-4   By Theodore J. Musho. Santa Costanza

CONSISTENCY

Discipline in drawing is sometimes associated with stiff or spartan-looking drawings. But, as you can see, quality need not be a limit to expression. These drawings have their internal consistency in common. It might be compared to the differences in car designs. The Porsche and the Lincoln Continental are immediately recognized as two very different cars, but both have an expression of high quality and craftsmanship. Given the basic concept of each car, the designers have given every part of the car a feeling that it belongs to that, and only that car.

STYLE AND SELECTIVITY

Architects often develop certain "trademarks" in their drawings as their careers develop. The resulting style of the sketches can be seen as a reflection of the designer's personality: tentative lines might indicate a willingness to remain open to new ideas whereas more deliberate delineation might show the designer's preference for deliberateness and quick closure on decisions.

Style is also formed by the architect's consistent selection of what he wants to show in his sketches and what he wants to leave out. His choices are often a reflection of what he feels are important design concerns in most projects.

9-5   By LeCorbusier. Baghdad Gymnasium

9-6   By Oscar Niemeyer. Capanema Residence

ENERGY AND VITALITY

Sketches, such as the ones to the right, project the enthusiasm and intensity of the act of putting the images on paper. The design and realization of a building can be a taxing experience particularly for the client. We know that the architect can help by instilling confidence and a sense of optimism. Vitality in sketches can do a lot to reinforce what we say to clients or others working on a project.

154

9-7   By Jim Anderson. Country Side YMCA,
        Landplus West Inc., Landscape Architects

9-8   By Lawrence Halprin. Lovejoy Plaza and Cascade,
        Portland, Oregon

9-9   By Edwin F. Harris, Jr. Pisan Group

9-10   By Gerald Exline.

Pisan Group

CREATIVITY AND REFRESHMENT

If we accept the premise that architects are creative in solving problems and open to new ways of seeing environment, the importance of a creative quality in our drawings should be obvious. As much as people strive to make decisions on an informed, rational basis, information is sometimes incomplete and there is usually a degree of risk-taking involved in design. Risks are taken on the basis of expectations which, in part, are conveyed by the way the architect expresses himself in his sketches.

DIRECTION AND FOCUS

A team of creative people working on a design problem need to have an understanding of the general direction and parameters of their efforts while being given a sense of freedom and flexibility to fully contribute to the success of the project. Some architects are able to meet these needs in preliminary conceptual sketches. Tom Larson explains it this way, "These drawings are not yet 'architecture' intentionally. I am beginning to carve out negative space, to begin to understand the organizing spaces of the project. These are quick drawings."

9-15   By Hugh Stubbins. Mount Holyoke College
Dormitories

9-16   Paddack Residence Study

CHARACTER AND MOOD

For many architects, one of the most difficult
problems in design is the representation, the
'capturing' of the intended character of a
space or object. Here again, the way sketches
are drawn can be of great help. On these two
pages, I have tried to gather examples of a
wide range of moods communicated by way of
sketches. The skills demonstrated here as
well as in the preceding pages, are those of
observation as much as manual skills. Sketching is supported by thinking and the sketches
reflect experiences.

Part II
Graphic Thinking and
Design Processes

PROGRAM   DESIGN   BUILD

client architect contractor

users
management
finance
legal affairs
public affairs
sales

planner
landscape architect
industrial designer
cost surveyor
architect
mechanical engineer
electrical engineer
structural engineer
specialist

manufacturers
suppliers
contractor
sub-contractor
construction manager

unions

land developer
realator
building process manager
anthropologist
sociologist

building system developer

construction finance

162

10 Design Process

In these last three chapters, we will aim at a better understanding of the processes of design for the individual, the team, and the public, and how graphic thinking skills can be applied.

It is clear that our profession is undergoing a revolution involving fundamental change and fundamental continuity. Architecture has traditional methods which are important to environmental problem-solving; but the scope of recognized environmental problems is expanding rapidly. There are two evident choices: expand the concept of the profession to encompass the full scope of emerging needs or achieve a new unity of professional activity under another label like environmental design. Either way, these changes call for the reassessment of communication in design processes.

Changes in processes of designing and building are immediately evident: more actors are involved at all stages; these actors are part of, and therefore influenced by, other professional or business contexts. The manufacturer must look beyond any single building or development for his ongoing concerns about marketing, production, and supplies. The zoning board must consider a building project within the context of an ongoing process of mediating public and private interests in the use of land.

Three important conditions for design are overlaying this complex network of actors and activities.

1. Change in the concept of clients, to include building users and/or the public.
2. Expansion of the "design team" to include clients, contractors, manufacturers, researchers, etc. as the project requires.
3. Increase in the number and complexity of concerns which shape the design and building processes.

This presents a new set of challenges foreseeable on three different scales:

1. Individual—The challenge of developing an ability to communicate rapidly with ourselves on increasingly complex problems, in a way which accepts their complexity while trying to see them in comprehensive, systemic terms.
2. Team—The challenge of communicating to motivate, to share goals, and to bring the fullest impact of each team member's expertise and concerns on the problems.
3. Public—The challenge of developing communication methods that cross the boundaries of traditional professional language to allow the public equal access to the

designing and building process. It is my belief that graphic thinking will be a major asset in meeting these communication challenges, if we are willing to develop the necessary skills.

A DESIGN PROCESS

Regardless of what is being designed or who is involved in designing it, there is a common objective: translating the client's program into a specific building or another response to his needs. In architectural practice this normally involves the following steps: building program, schematic design, preliminary design, design development, contract documents, shop drawings, construction. At each of these steps, the problems that must be solved require from the designer an effective problem-solving process. There are many good models for problem-solving processes. I prefer the following five-step model:

1. *Problem definition* Identifying the specific limits of the problem to be solved. Then, the various parts of the problem are analyzed to determine needs, constraints, and resources. Finally, the designer sets up specific design objectives.
2. *Developing alternatives* The designer examines existing and new solutions and develops several viable alternatives.
3. *Evaluation* Design evaluation criteria are adopted on the basis of the design objectives. Then the alternative solutions are rated using the design criteria.
4. *Selection* Based on the results of the evaluation, one alternative is selected. If no one alternative is clearly superior, two or more solutions may be combined. In either case, the chosen alternative is usually further modified using some of the more successful parts of the other solutions.
5. *Communication* The final solution to the problem must be described in such a way as to make it usable for the next stage of design.

This model is not as complex as it might seem initially. Take an example from the preliminary design stage:

1. The specific problem is the enclosure of a living space for a house. Needs include views, air circulation, sun control, and access to the exterior. Constraints include the overall plan and orientation of the house, the position of elements in the living space, and the climatic conditions impacting on the space. Among the resources are the construction technique, materials, and enclosure prototypes. The specific design objectives are: provide a panoramic view of the southwest while seated by the fireplace; shield the room from the intense summer sun, especially from the west but allow the winter sun to penetrate and heat most of the area; provide for easy access to the exterior deck; assure security of the area at night

2. The alternatives developed are: a conventional arrangement of windows and a door; sliding doors with a roll-down protective door; a glazed wall with a sun screen

3. Comparing the alternatives, the sun screen provides the best control of light but obscures the view, the conventional arrangement allows a view but does not control the sun or provide nightime security. The roll-down door provides security but does not control the sun.

4. The roll-down door is selected but without floor to ceiling glazing and a partial screen is used to control the sun

5. To make a final decision before the design can proceed to the next stage, all the important sketches of the enclosure must be completed

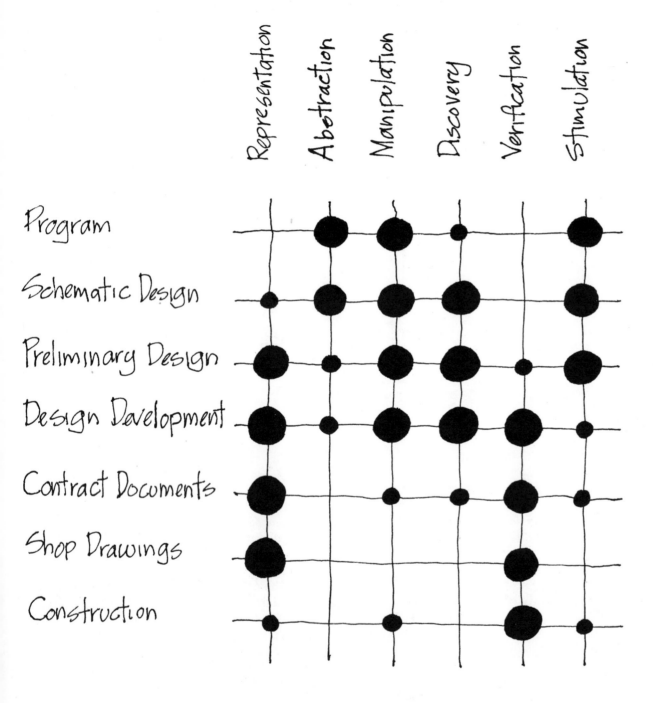

APPLYING GRAPHIC THINKING

Although the drawings which sum up each stage in the design process vary from abstract sketches at the beginning to the most specific hard-line drawings at the end, the thinking process can be supported throughout by the different types of sketches presented in the previous chapters. The matrix to the left shows where the modes of graphic thinking are primarily useful. To the right are some examples of the sketches which could be used at each of the stages in the design process.

The following chapters will consider some of the practical problems of creative thinking encountered by people within their design processes. I will try to show how some of the graphic thinking tools have been helpful to architects and designers, but the real test of the usefulness of these tools will have to be made within the context of the special design processes which each of us develops.

Program

Schematic Design

Preliminary Design

Design Development

Contract Documents

Shop Drawings

Construction

11-1   By Alvar Aalto.

11 Individual Design

The development and support of individual design thinking is best promoted by the individual designer. To be effective, each designer must be comfortable with his own method of thinking; this means that he must carefully select the methods, tools, and environment best suited to his special style of thinking. This chapter looks at alternative styles and some of the means for supporting effective thinking.

ABSTRACT TO CONCRETE THINKING

Graphic thinking is most effective when it respects basic thinking processes. "Thinking processes actually are automatic, swift and spontaneous when allowed to proceed undisturbed by other influences. Therefore what we need is to be educated in how not to interfere with the inherent capacity of the human mind to think."[1] For this reason, the media and type of drawings used by architects for graphic thinking (most of the drawings in this book) differ significantly from the drafted, "hardline" drawings usually associated with architectural design. Graphic thinking sketches must be rapid, flexible and unrestrictive to thinking processes.

Within the range of these sketches, there are two basic tendencies: exploratory abstract sketches and definitive concrete sketches. These respond to two types of thinking. "The first is fast, crude, holistic, and parallel, while the second is deliberate, attentive, detailed and sequential."[2] Designers generally lean toward one or the other of these types of thinking and probably use a little of both. To increase effectiveness, each designer should be aware of his basic type of thinking and be able to recognize when the other type is appropriate.

169

Private

PRIVATE TO PUBLIC THINKING

Thinking and the communication it may require has two modes. In the *public* mode, the individual develops his ideas by communicating with other people. "Communication is essentially a social affair. . . . The very word 'communicate' means 'share,' and in as much as you and I are communicating at this moment, we are one. . . . what we share, we cannot each have as our own possession, . . ."[3] In this sense, there is a public aspect to all ideas since none of us lives in a vacuum. What we hold in our mind comes from interactions with the people and environment that surrounds us.

In the *private* mode of thinking, the individual develops ideas in isolation of others; communication in this form is directed back towards oneself. Many architects are reluctant to show the sketches they use to develop ideas and some, even have difficulty discussing them. These sketches are tentative and crude compared to presentation drawings and they often

Semi-Private

Public

11-4   By Thomas Beeby. Studies for the Seyfarth House

11-5   By David Stieglitz. Buffalo Waterfront Redevelopment Project

represent incomplete thoughts. But these sketches also reveal a lot of struggle, a mind that doesn't have all the answers. For some designers, this might be embarrassing because of an illusion that the great design concepts flow instantly and completely from the creative mind. But perhaps, there is more to it. Conceptual sketches are very personal statements, almost a diary. We are intuitively aware that they can reveal very private feelings, concerns, or fantasies. They are no one else's business.

Although individual design activity requires both public and private communications, the choice of mode is personal. Each designer develops his own style of sketching as an aid to thinking. Some may choose to develop a clarity that can communicate to other people while others may develop a private graphic language. Either way, you have to be comfortable with it. If you can enjoy sketching, chances are thinking will also be more enjoyable.

DESIGN AS A LIFETIME PROCESS

Design methodology has some difficulties, such as its focus on the single project and presenting a rather mechanical model of design work. It gives the impression that the information is poured in at the beginning and at strategic points along the way; then the machine, called *logical thought,* grinds and chews the information, expelling an appropriate product at the end. The actual complexity of the design process might be better understood if we imagine the machine as having several switches to make the individual parts stop and go, speed up or slow down. Furthermore, each switch has a control that flips the switch back and forth at random. These controls represent the action of the human mind within a design process, for our mind is constantly active and reacting to a whole environment surrounding a specific project. In many cases, the design process of a successful architect becomes understandable when seen as one small part of the architect's life. His design process is governed by patterns of thought, interests, and values that are constantly evolving.

Graphic thinking can be a significant aid to such development. Charles Jencks noted of

PROJECT PROCESS

LIFE-TIME PROCESS

Blossom House

Unity Temple

Winslow House

Falling
Water

LeCorbusier, "He started keeping a sketch-book, a pocket-sized writing pad, to jot down ideas, visual impressions and anecdotes. These sketchbooks, of which there are more than seventy covering the whole of LeCorbusier's life, were in themselves a significant addition to Jeanneret's development, for they became a new medium of expression and a source-book for later ideas." Jencks goes on to quote LeCorbusier. "When one travels and works with visual things—architecture, painting, sculpture—one uses one's eyes and *draws,* so as to fix deep down in one's experience what is seen. Once the impression has been recorded by the pencil, it stays for good, entered, registered, inscribed."[4]

Creative architects often become fascinated with a particular problem or form which they will mull over for many years, drawn toward what they feel are fundamental ideas or con-cerns. For example, Wright pursued many notions in his lifetime regarding such things as plan organization, structure, materials which he could pull together in a single design such as the Kaufman House at Falling Water. In effect, the success of this house is the result of very thorough research.

PREPARATION FOR DESIGNING

Although thoughts can be represented graphically by using a great number of media (and there are whole books devoted to these different media), each designer must find materials and instruments with which he will be most comfortable. It is worthwhile to experiment with these different tools. They should be easy to use and maintain, and be portable. Personally, I prefer pens to pencils because they produce a high-contrast image, making it easy to get a consistent line quality. They are permanent which discourages the time-consuming habits of erasing or redrawing. I have found three types of pen that meet my needs:

Liquid ink cartridge pen—Using permanent, jet-black ink, it produces a smooth quick line. Most points will wear out eventually so I use cheap pens with fine rounded points and keep several handy in case one wears out.

Pointed Felt-Tip pen—This used to be the most common type felt-tip. It has the advantage of providing a second line weight by using the side of the point, but the ink often thins out, resulting in less sharp images.

Fine-point felt-tip pen—Many of these pens have a thin metal tube that greatly reduces the wear and mishaping of the point. Look for the pens with the darkest black ink.

For good results the drawing instrument must be matched with the right paper. Although the liquid cartridge pen will work on most papers, the non-porous, smooth finish paper is the most adaptable for all pens. I buy cheap, white ditto paper in 8½ by 11 size, 500 sheet packages. My test for an acceptable match of pen and paper is whether the pen can be moved quickly in any direction without catching or skipping.

Many architects get good results with soft pencils or colored pencils, and some combine media. Everyone's interests and thinking differs, so each person should try to find a simple but effective media for their graphic thinking.

ENVIRONMENT

It is curious that architects, whose profession is concerned with suiting environments to needs, spend little time studying the environment in which they work. Robert McKim provides us with a good description: "A visual-thinking environment for one person should be as well-designed as a contemporary kitchen. Work areas should be well-illuminated, preferably with natural north light and without shadow or glare. The drawing surface should be large and adjustable in height and angle. An additional stand-up table should be available for three-dimensional work; spilled glue and knife marks soon spoil a drawing surface. Organized storage should be provided close to each work area to diminish distracting clutter. Chairs and stools should provide back support in a working position. To alleviate back tension, and also to provide for the important element of change, a stand-up, vertical drawing surface should be available: a blackboard, easel, or wall-mounted roll of paper. A large tack-space is needed for displaying current idea-sketches. Althought admittedly an affront to those who associate productive work with open eyes and erect position, the visual thinker should also have access to a quiet place where he can relax and turn his thoughts inward—or stop thinking entirely: a reclining chair, a couch, even a relaxing bath!"[5]

Architects and designers should consciously select the visual environment in which they work to complement their own style of thinking. I find that my own development makes me responsive to everything visible. I support concentration by using a clear desk with a blank white vertical surface directly in front of me. Other designers may need a very stimulating environment for thinking.

MENTAL/PHYSICAL CONDITION

The right materials and environment must be accompanied by a good mental and physical state for the individual to think or solve problems effectively. Everyone is subject to tension and stress in their work, and this is especially true of practicing architects. Experienced architects try to pace themselves because they know that mistakes are made under excessive pressure. Frequent exercise and recreation are a basis for good mental state but designers can also take specific measures to improve their preparation for work. Relax eyes by closing then rotating them, ease neck tension by sitting upright with back supported and slowly bend the head forward, backward, and to each side in a circular motion, relax the whole body by stretching and deep breathing.

OBSTACLE 1.

OBSTACLE 2

OVERCOMING OBSTACLES

Even the best preparation does not assure success in design. Architectural students and, sometimes even, practitioners run into thinking and problem-solving obstacles. The following list describes some of the more common obstacles and some possible responses.

1. *Can't get started*—If you try to tackle problems that are too big, you become overwhelmed. Try to break down the problem into different parts. Instead of de-

signing the whole school, analyze its parts: classrooms, recreation, administration, etc . . . When these problems are under control, look at how the parts can fit together to form a school.

2. *Can't get any good ideas*—Sometimes there is a sense of "fear of failure", afraid that our solution will be judged very poor by others and that they will lose confidence in us. This requires separating one's self from the design problem. If failures in life meant that our life was a failure, we would all be in deep trouble. Fortunately, life goes on

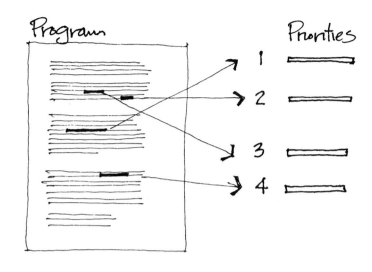

OBSTACLE 3.

OBSTACLE 4.

and this problem will soon be forgotten. The future holds difficult problems as well as easier ones. It may help to treat the problem as a challenge in a game. Try your best and use all of the resources available. Use some of the techniques of manipulation already discussed and take a new look at the problem. If you cannot move ahead on the basis of your assumptions, then arbitrarily change these assumptions. If there doesn't seem to be a suitable solution for the kitchen, consider a house without a formal kitchen. It may not be a solution, but it might lead to a solution.

3. *Can't make a decision*—Sometimes designers cannot progress on a project because they find it difficult to come to conclusions or decide on a course of action. Choices can be facilitated by spelling out the available alternatives and then comparing them in light of a few basic criteria. Representing criteria and the ratings of alternatives in graphic images makes it possible to have a picture of the information needed to decide.

4. *Can't finish*—Once a design instructor advised that if we were working under pressure and heard a tapping sound, we

should stop and see if it was ourselves dotting in the grass on our drawing. He said this was a sure sign that we were avoiding a critical problem in the design. If you find that you are filling up time or just going through the motions, it may help to go back to the original program or problem statement and ask what are the basic design objectives, what must the design achieve minimally not to be a failure. The chances are you will find the deficiency and save yourself a lot of trouble later on.

Agency

School

N

Service

Institute

Newspaper

Industry

Community Center

General Hospital

Medical Institute

12 Team Design

Although a great portion of this book deals with individual design thinking, in our world, design rarely takes place in isolation. "In the nature of architectural design, it is not possible for any architect to wield power without the full collaboration of others. With very few exceptions, the architect inevitably works as a member of a group; however strong his personality, he still needs a great many other people—architects, technicians, consultants, contractors, and so on—to translate his ideas into reality."[1]

The project-based design team has been one of the major features of the modern American architectural firm. Offices such as Skidmore Owings and Merril, The Architects Collaborative, and Caudill Rowlett Scott contributed significantly to the development of the team concept. They demonstrated that problem-oriented teams have several advantages:

1. Much more expertise than possessed by the individual architect can be brought to bear on the project.
2. A wider range of building types can be tackled.
3. More creative thinking can be stimulated through teamwork.

4. A firm has a better chance of survival when it is based upon a principal of organization rather than the personality of a single architect.

The team concept has expanded well beyond the limits of the traditional architectural design team. Teams now include clients, users of the intended building, contractors, financiers, social scientists, manufacturers and specialists. We have learned that the success of a design often depends on all of their inputs.

TEAM COMMUNICATION

Graphic communication can play a very important part in the success of teamwork. To be effective, team members must constantly share information and ideas. With the use of graphic thinking skills, these contributions can be quickly presented to the group and remain always available for retrieval and manipulation. In addition, drawings help knock down the barriers built by the professional jargon thereby allowing persons of different disciplines to communicate as exemplified on the facing page with a project team that includes an architect, a planner, a systems engineer, and a transportation specialist.

Scientific research has recognized the importance of a "research community"; sharing of thoughts as the scientists pursue the same problem. Chemistry, for example, has evolved a graphic language that shares a broad range of ideas over complex problems. The graphic description of the DNA molecule is a dramatic example of the importance of the integration of graphics and thinking (a). The double-helix structure of the DNA molecule was hailed as a major breakthrough, opening up a whole new era of research in organic chemistry. Graphic thinking has aided the DNA research in several ways:

1. A model of the central object of research that is useful and acceptable to all of the research community.

2. A model presenting new challenges and problems to be solved.
3. A model providing a direction for individual researchers to continue work in their different areas of specialization.

Currently, several architectural firms are developing graphic techniques to assist design teams. The firm of Caudill Rowlett Scott is a leader in team communication. In *Architecture by Team* William Caudill explains the graphic techniques used by CRS teams to analyze problems, generate solutions, and evaluate results (b). He stresses: "Once there are empathy and communication among members, the team will move and every member will benefit. Without the two, people cannot work together. Without the two, there is no team."[2]

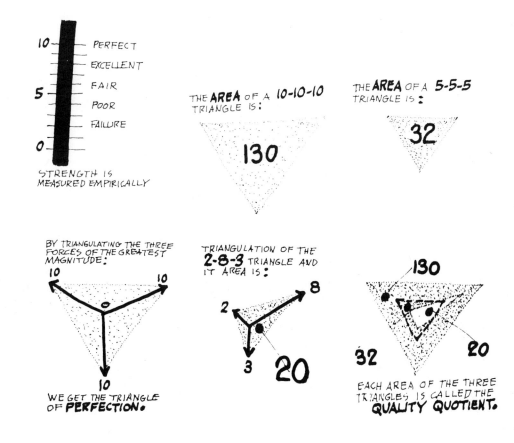

10 ─ PERFECT

   ─ EXCELLENT

   ─ FAIR

5 ─ POOR

   ─ FAILURE

0 ─

STRENGTH IS
MEASURED EMPIRICALLY

THE **AREA** OF A 10-10-10
TRIANGLE IS:

130

THE **AREA** OF A 5-5-5
TRIANGLE IS:

32

BY TRIANGULATING THE THREE
FORCES OF THE GREATEST
MAGNITUDE:

10   10

10

WE GET THE TRIANGLE
OF **PERFECTION.**

TRIANGULATION OF THE
2-8-3 TRIANGLE AND
IT AREA IS:

2   8

3   20

130

32   20

EACH AREA OF THE THREE
TRIANGLES IS CALLED THE
QUALITY QUOTIENT.

Obstruct through views from outside the site

Infill & intensification vs Removal & loss of density

Casual Supervision of children

Separate identities within the Project

Shifts in apartment sizes

1 br.

2 br.

3 br.

Family Groupings

APPLYING GRAPHICS

Graphic notation can contribute to team design by illustrating two important needs: information and processes of working toward a solution of the design problem. Most of the information needed to complete the design is included in the *design brief;* this term is distinguishable from the building *program* which in turn might be confused with *program* of functions. The design brief includes all of the information useful to the designing of the building.

the program of functions
description of users
client's objectives
financial constraints
time constraints
zoning restrictions
site analysis
site access
macro climate
micro climate
building prototypes
special planning considerations
construction system

The diagrams and sketches on these two pages illustrate some of the ways information from the design brief can be presented to the whole team.

Zoning Set-backs

EL. 100.00

EL. 150.00

Hierarcy of Dwelling Units

Inward oriented Atrium

alley

Vehicular Access to Site

VIEW

N

Terraced Housing

12-5, 6   Analysis card examples

BARCHART

NETWORK

BARCHART SHOWING PRECEDENCE

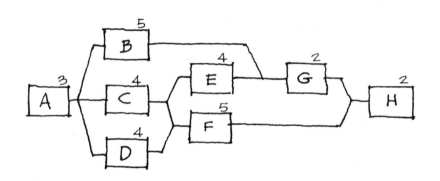

TASK-ORIENTED NETWORK

TEAM DESIGN PROCESS—MAKING A NETWORK

When many people must work together, it is often helpful to make a flowchart of all the tasks and where they come into context of the entire project. These networks evolved from simple bar charts (a) which show a simple schedule of tasks. By showing the necessary sequence of tasks (b), the basis is laid for an elementary network (c).

Networks can become quite elaborate if they include the most minute tasks, but I prefer to keep them simple in order to concentrate on the most basic activities. This simple network becomes a sort of rack on which to hang descriptions of information needed for different tasks (d). Since complex buildings or complex design processes require changes in team composition at different project stages, a network is also a handy way to identify points at which special expertise is needed (e).

12-7   Evolution of the process network diagram

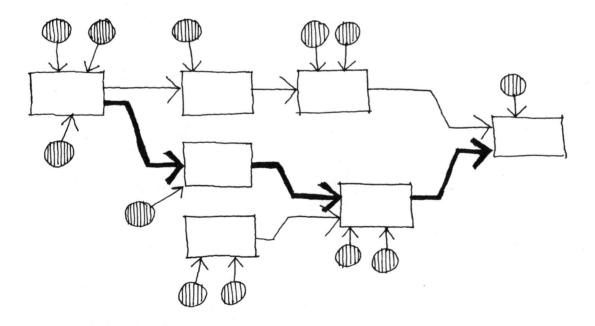

12–8a   A simplified network

12–8b   Attachment of information to the network

PROBLEM: BETTER STUDIOS
- more tack surface
- sense of studio identity
- lighting

Objective:
- more student interaction
- current display of work
- social atmosphere

Put aside visual studio models

what can we see

1.

Restaurant Analogy
eating & conversation
reduced tension

reduced light level

28"

What else is a studio like?

If I am a studio how do I behave? Welcoming Students

Reminds me of Paris cafes where they have a place for napkins for steady customers.

Bar could be the supply & services area

Good experience working in a corridor

5'0"   2'0"
Papers books   tack spaces

chairs on wheels

Class rooms offices etc   work shop   lounge relax

FORCE CIRCULATION PAST DESKS

2.

WE NEED SOMETHING MORE CRAZY!
how about a studio without drafting boards?

Original teaching was done outdoors

HOW ABOUT GARDEN HOT HOUSE

3.

TEAM CREATIVITY

Since graphic thinking increases the output of ideas for the individual, the possibilities for a group are geometrically increased, assuming that the way is opened for everyone to communicate. Alex Osborn[3] developed a method called *brainstorming* which helps to keep the channels of thinking open. He identified four rules that must be followed to generate ideas within a group during brainstorming:

1. Suspend judgment on anyone's idea,
2. Free-wheel, let your imagination roam,
3. Strive for quantity of ideas,
4. Build on each others ideas.

If one member of the brainstorming group concentrates on producing sketches of the ideas generated, the already-fertile situation is even more intensified as they feed back information to all members of the group. The number of possible new associations is at least doubled. The sketches should be as quick and loose as the ones shown here. Remember that only a simple recognizable symbol for the idea is required; in some instances this might be a word or phrase.

EVOLVING TEAM TECHNIQUES

Team thinking is an evolving area of research in creativity. New approaches are continually tested and visual communication could play an important role in realizing the potential of teams. As technological advances (graphic simulation and reproduction) improve, the speed of graphic manipulation and feedback is greatly increased. The possibilities are indeed exciting.

Making useful and practical advances in team thinking depends on the quality of relationship between the team members. A few suggestions may help:

1. Acceptance of each others contribution to the situation as having equal potential.
2. Place personal goals below the team goals.
3. Help each other by concentrating on each member's input.
4. Have your sense of humor ready and use it.

13-1   Public oriented graphics from the Athens,
Ohio Urban Design Study, P. Laseau and
G. K. Nishi

13 Public Design

The general public is taking a more active role in design of individual communities and people are working more closely with design professionals. Graphic thinking has changed to accomodate this new development. This chapter will discuss the fundamental shifts in the public's attitude and show how these shifts support design and problem-solving processes.

Explorers of the fifteenth and sixteenth centuries verified the newly introduced concept about the shape of the earth and this changed forever man's sense of relationship to his world. In our century, explorers of the universe added another dimension with the concept of the earth as a "spaceship", a wonderously brilliant island floating in the vast blackness of space. Once again the impact of our concept of relationship to our environment, the earth, has and will have fundamental consequences. Other dramatic changes have altered our view of the world: horse and buggy to rocketships; musket to atomic annihilation; telecommunications; mini-computers; energy crisis; large-scale pollution of air and water; electric power failures; etc . . .

Books such as *The Age of Discontinuity, Future Shock,* and *The Temporary Society*[1]

have attempted to describe these shifts in values. The student revolution of the late sixties outwardly reflected the change in values. In the area of architecture and environmental design, the shift in values is most dramatically expressed in the historic preservation movement. Now, that changes have become a central feature in our lives, people are beginning to exercise their judgment over which changes are desirable and which are not. They are developing new perceptions about historical buildings as sources of continuity in communities. They seem to seek stability in an atmosphere of overwhelming change.

I believe that we are seeking a new sense of identity for ourselves and our community. The increased value placed on the environment is already having important effects on our economic system; companies are searching for locations with a great influx of people rather than moving people to where the jobs are. Early successful design responses to the preservation movement as in Ghirardelli Square and the Cannery [2] in San Francisco have been followed by a wave of rediscovery and preservation movements in the main streets of towns across the country. Community development associations are springing up

One-Way Communication   vs   Two-Way Communication

everywhere as consumer movements convince an increasing number of people that they can personally do something to improve their lives and their environment.

COMMUNITY DESIGN

Architects must work more directly with the public to avoid the mistakes of the past. "Some of the environmental changes . . . have had negative impacts that were not easily discernible at first. They *seemed* to be good things to do—to relocate a museum or provide new housing or put a sports arena in a park. What happened eventually was that the museum lost participants, the housing was disliked, the park patrons shunned the sports facilities. The reason for these kinds of failures is usually that the changes broke connections between people and the opportunities their community offered."[3] The best way to assure that people are not cut off from community opportunities is to involve them in the design of their communities.

If the architect is to promote the involvement of the public in the design process, he must take a look at the way ideas are communicated. Some architects are accustomed to making highly-polished presentations to clients or

13-3a, b   Contrast in approaches to design communication
13-4   Freehand drawing done over a drafted version

13-5   By Harry Eggink. Local retail street, East
        Cambridge Study
13-6   By Harry Eggink. East Cambridge residential
        neighborhood

boards of directors. Their drawings are slick
with an air of finality and certainty. When such
drawings are used in a public participation
design project, the average person has the
feeling he is being talked at and not talked
with; he is intimidated and discouraged from
contributing his ideas no matter how much
to the contrary the designer pleads. Inviting
communication starts with the character of
the sketches.

1. Sketches should always have a loose free-
    hand quality, a sort of incompleteness
    suggesting that they can be changed and
    will be improved with additional thinking.
    Even if a perspective has been mechani-
    cally constructed, it can be traced over
    freehand to achieve a more tentative
    feeling.
2. Keep sketches simple and avoid abstrac-
    tions which require interpretation. The
    examples, on the right, from a Cambridge
    urban design study[4] are quite effective.
    Many people find it easier to relate to
    aerial views.
3. Use many labels to easily identify the
    parts of the drawings. The cartoon caption
    bubble is a useful device for labeling or
    conveying the possibilities of an environ-
    ment.

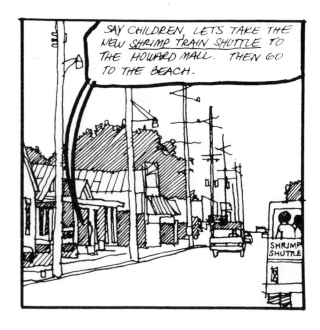

TAKE PART WORKSHOPS

Several architects and planners are working vigorously to develop graphic communication methods making it possible for the public to understand and enter into the design process. One of the innovators in this trend is Lawrence Halprin. "I am concentrating on the issue of people's interactions with their environment both as individuals *and* in groups. . . . both aspects are important. We have been searching for archetypal relationships . . . in workshops which take place primarily out in the field. These *taking part* workshops allow people the

opportunity to discover and articulate their own needs and desires for themselves and for their communities. . . . they discover ways of communicating with each other and arriving at creative decisions based on multiple input."[5]

Jim Burns, a planning consultant and former Halprin associate with wide experience in organizing workshops, describes the workshop process as having four basic steps:

1. Awareness—Community members get a better experience of those things which form the community environment and how

those things are interconnected. Awareness is achieved principally by going out into the community and looking and taking notes.

2. Perception—Citizens begin to understand their community and their personal relationship to it by modeling the collective experience of what exists and their hopes for what could exist.

3. Decision-Making—Based on awareness and perceptions the community describes what they would like done and when it should be done.

transit loop

Bay

BAYVIEW AVE

DIVISION ST

HOWARD AVE

ROUTE 90

Mississippi Sound

0 Feet 3000

1. WALKWAY. 2. PASSAGE THROUGH OLD BLDG. WITH OFFICES OVER. 3. APARTMENTS OVER COMMERCIAL.

4. Implementation—Strategies are devised to assure that the projects adopted by the community are realized.[6]

To complete these four steps, workshops have developed a number of graphic aids (adjoining illustrations) to involve the community members in the design process.

13–12   By Peter Hasselman. Atlantic City Study

13–13   By John J. Desmond. Phoenix Study

AMERICAN INSTITUTE OF ARCHITECTS—REGIONAL/URBAN DESIGN ASSISTANCE TEAM

For more than ten years the American Institute of Architects has been sending teams of professionals into communities to conduct urban design studies. These teams, which include architects, economists, urban designers, sociologists, managers, and lawyers, work with resource persons from the community to analyze problems and develop strategies. An important part of the R/UDAT (Regional/Urban Design Assistance Team)[7] process is the report they give to the whole community on the findings of the joint professional-citizen team. It is critical to future progress of community development that the public understand that the report is only a suggestion for an approach to development and not the description of a final product. The sketches used in the report to the community attempt to give general images of environmental objectives without proposing specific design solutions. They provide us with models for public design communication.

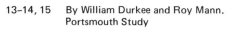

13–14, 15   By William Durkee and Roy Mann.
            Portsmouth Study

13–16   By Charles A. Blessing. Phoenix Study

PHOENIX CORE

14 Conclusion

Architecture and the other arts hold a vital place in the future of our culture, creativity being one of the most important factors. Looking over this book, it occurs to me that the bulk of what is written deals with how or what could be done and not so much with why.

The importance of the arts to national survival was pointed out clearly in the 1951 "Massey Report" commissioned by the Canadian Government: "When Mr. Churchill in 1940 called the British people to their supreme effort, he invoked the traditions of his country, and based his appeal on the common background from which had grown the character and the way of life of his fellow countrymen. In the spiritual heritage of Great Britain was found the quickening force to meet the menacing facts of that perilous hour. Nothing could have been more 'practical' than that appeal to thought and emotion. . . . Canada became a national entity because of certain habits of mind and convictions which its people shared and would not surrender. Our country was sustained through difficult times by the power of this spiritual legacy. It will flourish in the future in proportion as we believe in ourselves. It is the intangibles which give a nation not only its essential character but its vitality as well. What may seem unimportant or even irrelevant under the pressure of daily life may well be the thing that endures, which may give a community its power to survive. But tradition is always in the making and from this fact we draw a second assumption: the innumerable institutions, movements, and individuals interested in the arts, letters and sciences throughout our country are now forming the national tradition of the future."[1]

Architects *are* problem solvers, but the problems of architecture like the problems of our society run much deeper than the so-called "practical" level. A building should reinforce the spirit as well as provide safety and security. Architecture must still be an *art* and a *science.*

Notes

Preface

1. From "The Need of Perception for the Perception of Needs", keynote speech by Dr. Heinz Von Foerster delivered at the 1975 National Convention of the American Institute of Architects, Atlanta, Georgia.

Chapter 1

1. Broadbent, Geoffrey. *Design in Architecture.* New York: John Wiley & Sons, Inc., 1973, p. 343.

2. Hamilton, Edward A. *Graphic Design for the Computer Age.* New York: Van Nostrand Reinhold Company, 1970, p. 16.

3. McKim, Robert H. *Experiences in Visual Thinking.* Monterey, Calif.: Brooks/Cole, 1972, p. 22.

4. Arnheim, Rudolf. *Visual Thinking.* Berkeley, Calif.: University of California Press, 1969, p. 13.

5. Arnheim, Rudolf. "Gestalt Psychology and Artistic Form". In *Aspects of Form,* edited by Lancelot Law Whyte. Bloomington; Indiana University Press, 1966, p. 203.

6. McKim, *Experiences in Visual Thinking,* p. 40.

7. Arnheim, "Gestalt Psychology and Artistic Form", p. 206.

8. Levins, A. S. *Graphics.* New York: John Wiley & Sons, Inc., 1962, p. 415.

9. Arnheim, Rudolf. *Art and Visual Perception: A Psychology of the Creative Eye.* Berkeley, Calif.: University of California Press, 1954, p. 46.

Chapter 2

1. All of the successful architectural designers that I have interviewed, stressed the importance of sketching ability in their work.

2. Downer, Richard. *Drawing Buildings.* New York: Watson-Guptill Pubns., Inc., 1962, p. 9.

3. Perls, Frederick. *Ego, Hunger, and Aggression.* New York: Random House, 1969.

4. Cullen, Gordon. *Townscape.* London: The Architectural Press, 1961.

5. Gundelfinger, John. As quoted in *On-the-spot Drawing,* by Nick Meglin. New York: Watson-Guptill Pubns., Inc., 1969, p. 62.

6. Folkes, Michael. *Drawing Cartoons.* New York: Watson-Guptill Pubns., Inc., 1963, p. 19.

Chapter 3

1. *Websters New World Dictionary,* 2d ed. New York: William Collins & World Publishing Co., Inc., 1976.

2. Arnheim, *Art and Visual Perception: A Psychology of the Creative Eye,* p. 33.

3. Lockhard, William Kirby. *Design Drawing.* Tucson, Ariz.: Pepper Publishing, 1974, p. 124.

4. *Helmut Jacoby Architectural Drawings.* New York: Praeger Publishers, Inc., 1965.

5. Gundelfinger, *On-the-spot Drawing,* pp. 61–62.

6. Lockhard, *Design Drawing,* p. 262.

Chapter 4

1. Bonta, Juan Pablo. "Notes for a Semiotic Theory of Graphic Languages". Paper presented to the International Conference on Semiotics, Ulm, Germany, 1972.

2. McKim, *Experiences in Visual Thinking,* p. 129.

3. Bruner, Jerome. *On Knowing: Essays for the Left Hand.* Cambridge, Mass.: Belknap Press of Harvard University Press, 1962.

4. Arnheim, "Gestalt Psychology and Artistic Form", p. 204.

5. Bruner, *On Knowing: Essays for the Left Hand.*

6. McKim, *Experiences in Visual Thinking,* pp. 124–126.

Chapter 5

1. Best, Gordon. "Method and Intention in Architectural Design" published in *Design Methods in Architecture.* Edited by Geoffrey Broadbent, and Anthony Ward, New York: George Wittenborn, Inc., 1969, p. 155.

2. Broadbent, *Design in Architecture,* p. 365.

3. McKim, *Experiences in Visual Thinking,* p. 105.

4. McKim, *Experiences in Visual Thinking,* p. 127.

5. Rittel, Horst. "Some principles for the Design of an Educational System for Design". Part I, *DMG Newsletter,* Berkeley, Calif.: Design Methods Group, Dec. 1970.

6. Peña, William M. *Problem Seeking: An Architectural Programming Primer.* Boston: Cahners Books International, Inc., 1977, pp. 170–179.

Chapter 6

1. *The American Heritage Dictionary of the English Language.* New York: American Heritage Publishing Co., Inc., 1970.

2. Koberg, Don, and Bagnall, Jim. *The Universal Traveler.* Los Altos, Calif.: William Kaufmann, Inc., 1976, p. 9.

3. McKim, *Experiences in Visual Thinking,* p. 45.

4. Rowan, Helen. "The Creative People: How to Spot Them". *THINK,* New York: International Business Machines Corporation, Nov.–Dec. 1962, vol. 28, no. 10, p. 15.

5. Websters New World Dictionary

6. March, Lionel, and Steadman, Philip. *The Geometry of Environment.* London: RIBA Publications Limited, 1971, p. 28.

7. Beeby, Thomas H. "The Grammar of Ornament/Ornament as Grammar". *VIA III,* The Journal of the Graduate School of Fine Arts, University of Pennsylvania, 1978, p. 11.

8. Beeby, "The Grammar of Ornament/Ornament as Grammar", pp. 11–12.

9. Carl, Peter. "Towards a Pluralist Architecture." *Progressive Architecture.* Feb. 1973, p. 84.

10. Norberg-Schulz, C. *Existence, Space and Architecture.* New York: Praeger Publishers, Inc., 1971, p. 109.

11. Hanks, Kurt, Belliston, Larry, and Edwards, Dave. *Design Yourself.* Los Altos, Calif.: William Kaufmann, Inc., 1977, p. 112.

Chapter 7

1. Rowan, "The Creative People: How to Spot Them", p. 11.

2. Rowan, "Creative People: How to Spot Them", p. 13.

3. Pye, David. *The Nature of Design.* New York: Reinhold Publishing Corporation, 1964, pp. 65–66.

4. McKim, *Experiences in Visual Thinking,* p. 47.

5. Broadbent, *Design in Architecture,* p. 341.

6. Broadbent, *Design in Architecture,* p. 343.

7. Alexander, Christopher, Ishikawa, Sara, and Silverstein, Murray. *A Pattern Language.* New York: Oxford University Press, 1977, pp. xliii–xliv.

Chapter 8

1. Lockhard, *Design Drawing,* p. 119.

2. Peña, *Problem Seeking: An Architectural Programming Primer,* p. 165.

Chapter 11

1. Kubie, Lawrence. *Neurotic Distortion of the Creative Process.* Garden City, New York: Farrar, Straus & Giroux, Inc., (Noonday Press), 1961.

2. McKim, *Experiences in Visual Thinking,* p. 127.

3. Cherry, Colin. *On Human Communication.* Cambridge, Mass.: MIT Press, 1966, p. 4.

4. Jencks, Charles. *LeCorbusier and the Tragic View of Architecture.* Cambridge, Mass.: Harvard University Press, 1973.

5. McKim, *Experiences in Visual Thinking,* p. 31.

Chapter 12

1. Broadbent, *Design in Architecture,* p. 358.

2. Caudill, William W. *Architecture by Team.* New York: Van Nostrand Reinhold Company, 1971.

3. For a description of "brain storming" methods, see Gordon, William J. *Synetics: The Development of Creative Capacity.* New York: Macmillan Publishing Co., Inc., 1968.

Chapter 13

1. Drucker, Peter F. *The Age of Discontinuity.* New York: Harper & Row Pubs., Inc., 1968.
Toffler, Alvin. *Future Shock.* New York: Random House, 1970.
Bennis, Warren G., and Slater, Philip E. *The Temporary Society.* New York: Harper & Row Pubs., Inc., 1968.

2. These two renovation projects adapted large, older structures for use as shopping complexes in the waterfront area of San Francisco. They have both been very successful socially, aesthetically and economically.

3. Burns, Jim. *Connections: Ways to Discover and Realize Community Potentials.* Pittsburgh: Dowden, Hutchinson & Ross, Inc., 1979, p. 13.

4. Dowling, M. J., Eggink, H. A., Leish, B., and O'Riordan, J. *East Cambridge Study.* Cambridge, Mass.: The Graduate School of Design, Harvard University, 1976.

5. Halprin, Lawrence. *From Process: Architecture No. 4 Lawrence Halprin.* Edited by Ching-Yu Chang. Tokyo: Process Architects Publishing Company Ltd., 1978.

6. Burns, *Connections: Ways to Discover and Realize Community Potentials,* pp. 21–30.

7. The American Institute of Architects established the Regional/Urban Design Assistance Team Program several years ago as a service provided by the Profession for the public. In its short history, the program has served cities throughout our country with a combined population of over 10 million people.

Conclusion

1. *Report of the Royal Commission on National Development in the Arts, Letters and Sciences.* Ottawa, Canada: King's Printer, 1951.

Bibliography

I. DRAWING AND GRAPHICS

Atkin, William Wilson. *Architectural Presentation Techniques.* New York: Van Nostrand Reinhold Co., 1976.

Beittel, K. *Mind and Context in the Art of Drawing.* New York: Holt, 1972.

Bellis, Herbert F. *Architectural Drafting.* New York: McGraw Hill Book Co., 1971.

Bowman, William J. *Graphic Communication.* New York: John Wiley & Sons, Inc., 1968.

Ching, Frank. *Architectural Graphics.* New York: Van Nostrand Reinhold Co., 1975.

Collier, G. *Form, Space, and Vision.* Englewood Cliffs, New Jersey: Prentice-Hall Inc., 1972.

Czaja, Michael. *Freehand Drawing, Language of Design.* Walnut Creek, Calif.: Gambol Press, 1975.

DaVinci, Leonardo. *Notebooks.* New York: Dover Pub., Inc., 1970.

DeVries, Jan Vredeman. *Perspective.* New York: Dover Pub., Inc., 1968.

Downer, Richard. *Drawing Buildings.* New York: Watson-Guptill Pubns., Inc., 1962.

Dubery, Fred, and Willats, John. *Drawing Systems.* London: Van Nostrand Reinhold Co., 1972.

Goldstein, Nathan. *The Art of Responsive Drawing.* Englewood Cliffs, New Jersey: Prentice-Hall Inc., 1973.

Goodban, William T., and Hayslett, Jack. *Architectural Drawing and Planning.* New York: McGraw Hill Book Co., 1972.

Guptill, Arthur Leighton. *Drawing with Pen and Ink.* New York: Reinhold Pub. Co., 1961.

Hanks, Kurt, Belliston, Larry, and Edwards, Dave. *Design Yourself.* Los Altos, Calif.: William Kaufmann, Inc., 1977.

Hanks, Kurt, and Belliston, Larry. *Draw! A Visual Approach to Thinking, Learning, and Communicating.* Los Altos, Calif.: William Kaufmann, Inc., 1977.

Hayes, Colin. *Grammer of Drawing for Artists and Designers.* New York: Van Nostrand Reinhold Co., 1969.

Hill, Edward. *The Language of Drawing.* New York: Prentice-Hall Inc., 1966.

Hogarth, Paul. *Drawing Architecture: a creative approach.* New York: Watson-Guptill Pubns., Inc., 1973.

Jacoby, Helmut. *New Architectural Drawings.* New York: Praeger, 1969.

Jacoby, Helmut. *New Techniques of Architectural Rendering.* New York: Praeger, 1971.

Kemper, Alfred. *Presentation Drawings by American Architects.* New York: Wiley-Interscience, 1977.

Kliment, Stephen A. *Creative Communications for a Successful Design Practice.* New York: Watson-Guptill Pubns., Inc., 1977.

Lockhard, W. *Drawing as a Means to Architecture.* Reinhold, 1968.

Lockhard, William Kirby. *Design Drawing.* Tucson, Ariz.: Pepper Pub., 1975.

Lockhard, William Kirby. *Design Drawing Experiences.* Tucson, Ariz.: Pepper Pub., 1974.

Lockwood, Arthur. *Diagrams.* New York: Watson-Guptill Pubns., Inc., 1969.

McGinty, Tim. *Drawing Skills in Architecture.* Dubuque, Iowa: Kendall/Hunt Publishing Co., 1976.

Mendelowitz, David M. *A Guide to Drawing.* New York: Holt, Reinhart and Winston, 1976.

Murgio, Mathew. *Communication Graphics.* New York: Van Nostrand Reinhold Co., 1969.

Nicolaides, K. *The Natural Way to Draw.* Boston, Mass.: Houghton-Mifflin, 1941 (paperback ed. 1975).

North Carolina University. State College of Agriculture and Engineering. School of Design. *Student publication.* Vol. 14, Nos. 1–5, 1964–1965.

O'Connell, William J. *Graphic Communications in Architecture.* Champaign, Ill.: Stipes Pub. Co., 1972.

Pedretti, Carlo. *A Chronology of Leonardo DaVinci's Architectural Studies After 1500.* Geneva: E. Droz, 1962.

Röttger, Ernst, and Klante, Dieter. *Creative Drawing: Point and Line.* New York: Van Nostrand Reinhold Co., 1963.

Stegman, George K. *Architectural Drafting.* Chicago: American Technical Society, 1966.

Steinberg, Saul. *The Labyrinth.* New York: Harper & Brothers, 1960.

Thiel, Phillip. *Freehand Drawing, a primer.* Seattle: University of Wash. Press, 1965.

Thurber, James. *Thurber and Company.* New York: Harper & Row Pubs. Inc., 1966.

Walker, Theodore D. *Plan Graphics.* West Lafayette, Ind.: PDA Pub., 1975.

Weidhaas, Ernest R. *Architectural Drafting and Construction.* Boston: Allyn and Bacon, 1974.

White, Edward T. *Concept Sourcebook.* Tucson: Architectural Media, 1975.

II. DESIGN AND PROBLEM SOLVING

Adams, James L. *Conceptual Blockbusting.* New York: Scribner, 1974.

Alexander, Christopher. *Notes on the Synthesis of Form.* Cambridge: Harvard University Press, 1967.

Alexander, Christopher. Ishikawa, Sara, and Silverstein, Murray. *A Pattern Language.* New York: Oxford University Press, 1977.

Alger, J., and Hays, C. *Creative Synthesis in Design.* Englewood Cliffs, New Jersey: Prentice-Hall Inc., 1964.

Archer, L. Bruce. *The Structure of Design Processes.* London: Royal College of Art, 1968.

Bender, Tom G. *Environmental Design Primer.* New York: Schoken, 1976.

Best, Gordon. Method and Intention in Architectural Design. *Design Methods in Architecture* (Ed. by Broadbent and Ward). New York: George Wittenborn Inc., 1969.

Brinkers, H. *Decision-Making: Creativity. Judgement and Systems.* Columbus: Ohio State University, 1972.

Broadbent, Geoffrey. *Design in Architecture.* New York: John Wiley & Sons, Inc., 1973.

Burns, Jim. *Connections: Ways to Discover and Realize Community Potentials.* Pittsburgh: Dowden, Hutchinson & Ross, Inc., 1979.

Design Methods in Architecture Symposium. Broadbent, Geoffrey and Ward, Anthony (eds.). New York: G. Wittenborn, 1969.

Duffy, Francis, and Torrey, John. "A Progress Report on the Pattern Language" pp. 261–277. In Moore, Gary T. *Emerging Methods in Environmental Design and Planning.* Cambridge: MIT Press, 1970.

Emerging Methods in Environmental Design and Planning. Cambridge: Design Methods Group. MIT Press, 1968.

Environmental Design: Research and Practice. Environmental Design Research Conference. Los Angeles: University of California, 1972.

Garrett, L. *Visual Design, A Problem Solving Approach.* New York: Reinhold, 1967.

Halprin, Lawrence. *RSVP Cycles.* New York: George Braziller Inc., 1969.

Halprin, Burns. *Taking Part.* Cambridge: MIT Press, 1974.

Heimsath, Cloris. *Behavioral Architecture.* New York: McGraw Hill Book Co., 1977.

Jones, Owen. *The Grammer of Ornament.* London: B. Quaritch, 1910.

Jones, John Christopher. *Design Methods.* New York: Wiley-Interscience, 1920.

Koberg, Don, and Bagnall, Jim. *The Universal Traveler.* Los Altos, Calif.: William Kaufmann, Inc., 1972.

Manheim, Marvin L. *Problem Solving Processes in Planning and Design.* Cambridge: School of Engineering. MIT, 1967.

Mumford, Lewis. *The City in History.* New York: Harcourt, Brace & World, Inc., 1961.

Nelson, George. *Problems of Design.* New York: Whitney Pub., 1957.

Peña, William M. with Caudill, William W., and Focke, John W. *Problem Seeking.* Houston: Candill Rowlett Scott, 1969.

III. VISUAL COMMUNICATION AND PERCEPTION

Alexander, H. *Language and Thinking.* New York: Van Nostrand Reinhold Co., 1967.

Arnheim, Rudolf. *Visual Thinking.* Berkeley: Univ. California Press, 1969.

Bach, M. *Power of Perception.* Garden City, New York: Doubleday, 1966

Bartlett, F. C. *Remembering.* New York: Cambridge University Press, 1977.

Bartley, S. *Principles of Perception.* New York: Harper, 1972.

Block, H., and Salinger, H. *The Creative Vision.* Gloucester, Mass.: Peter Smith, 1968.

Bois, J. *The Art of Awareness.* Dubuque, Iowa: W. C. Brown, 1973.

Bry, Adelaide, and Bair, Marjorie. *Directing Movies of Your Mind: Visualization for Health and Insights.* New York: Harper and Row, 1978.

Chomsky, Noam. *Language and Mind.* New York: Harcourt Brace Jovanovich, 1972.

Chomsky, Noam. "Review of B. F. Skinner Verbal Behavior." *Language Magazine,* Jan–Mar 1959.

Cunningham, S., and Reagan C. *Handbook of Visual Perceptual Training.* Springfield, Il. Thomas, 1972.

Feldman, Edmund Burke. *Art As Image and Idea.* Englewood Cliffs, New Jersey: Prentice-Hall Inc., 1967.

Gibson, James. *The Perception of the Visual World.* Boston: Houghton-Mifflin, 1950.

Gibson, J. *The Senses Considered as Perceptual Systems.* Boston: Houghton-Mifflin, 1966.

Harlan, C. *Vision and Invention.* Englewood Cliffs, New Jersey: Prentice-Hall Inc., 1970

Hayakawa, S. *Language in Thought and Action.* New York: Harcourt Brace Jovanovich, 1978

Huxley, A. *The Art of Seeing.* Seattle, Wash.: Madrona Publishers, 1975.

Janson, H. W. *The Nature of Representation: A Phenomenological Enquiry* New York: New York University Press, 1961.

Jeanneret-Gris, Charles Edouard. *New World of Space.* New York: Reynal and Hitchcock, 1948.

Kepes, Gyorgy. *Language of Vision.* Chicago, Il.: Paul Theobold and Co., 1944.

Luckiesh, Matthew. *Visual Illusions, Their Causes, Characteristics and Applications.* New York: Dover, 1965.

McKim, Robert H. *Experiences in Visual Thinking.* Monterey, Calif.: Brooks/Cole, 1972.

The Notebook of Paul Klee. Vol. 1: The Thinking Eye. New York: Wittenborn, 1978.

Parameter, Ross. *The Awakened Eye.* Middletown, Conn.: Wesleyan University Press, 1968.

Pitcher, G. *A Theory of Perceptions.* Princeton, New Jersey: Princeton University, 1971.

Robertson, T. *Innovative Behavior and Communication.* New York: Holt, 1971.

Samuels, M. and Samuels, N. *Seeing with the Mind's Eye.* New York: Random House, 1975.

Sommer, Robert. *The Mind's Eye.* New York: Dell Publishing, 1978.

Vygotsky, Lev S. *Thought and Language.* Cambridge, Mass.: MIT Press, 1962.

Walker, Theodore D. *Perception and Environmental Design.* West Lafayette, Ind.: PDA Publishers, 1971.

Whitehead, Alfred North. *Symbolism, It's Meaning and Effect.* New York: Macmillan Co., 1959.

IV. CREATIVITY

Banker, W. *Brain Storms.* New York: Grove, 1968.

Barrett, W. *Time of Need: Forms of imagination in the 20th Century.* New York: Harper, 1972.

Batten, M. *Discovery By Chance.* New York: Funk and Wagnalls Co., 1968.

Berrill, N. J. *Man's Emerging Mind: The Story of Man's Progress Through Time.* New York: Fawcett World Library, 1965.

Boas, G. *History of Ideas.* New York: Scribners, 1969.

Bourne, L. *Human Conceptual Behavior.* Boston: Allyn and Bacon, 1966.

Brown, R. *The Creative Spirit.* Port Washington, New York: Kennikat, 1970.

Bruner, J., Goodnow, J., and Austin, G.: *A Study of Thinking.* New York: Wiley, 1956.

Burton, W., Kimball, R., and Wing, R. *Education for Effective Thinking.* New York: Appleton, 1960.

Chang, C. Y. *Creativity and Taoism.* New York: Harper, 1970.

Cobb, S. *Discovering the Genius Within You.* Metuchen, New Jersey: Scarecrow, 1967.

DeBono, E. *Lateral Thinking.* New York: Harper, 1972.

DeBono, E. *New Think.* New York: Basic Books, Inc., 1968.

Dyer, F., and Dyer, J. *Bureaucracy vs. Creativity.* Coral Gables: Univ. of Miami, 1965.

Eberle, R. Scamper: Games for Imaginative Development. Buffalo: D.O.K., 1972.

Garfield, Patricia. *Creative Dreaming.* New York: Ballantine Books, 1974.

Gombrich, E. H. *Art and Illusion.* New York: Phardon/Pantheon, 1960.

Gordon, W. J. J. *Synectics: The Development of Creative Capacity.* New York: Macmillan, 1968.

Greene, Herb. *Mind and Image.* Lexington, Kentucky: University Press of Kentucky, 1976.

Gruber, Howard E., ed. *Contemporary Approaches to Creative Thinking.* New York: Atherton Press, 1963.

Koestler, Arthur. *The Act of Creation: A Study of Conscious and Unconscious in Science and Art.* New York: Dell Publishing, 1973.

Korner, S. *Conceptual Thinking, a logical inquiry.* New York: Dover, 1959.

Krippner, S., and Hughes W. *Dreams and Human Potential.* Paper presented to American Association of Humanistic Psychology, 1969.

Maslow, A. H. *The Farther Reaches of Human Nature.* Paperback ed., New York: The Viking Press, 1973.

McKellar, Peter. *Imagination and Thinking: A psychological analysis.* Norwood Editions, Norwood Pa. 1978.

Osborn, A. F. *Applied Imagination: Principles and Practices of Creative Thinking.* New York: Scribners, 1957.

Pikas, A. *Abstraction and Concept Formation.* Cambridge: Harvard University, 1966.

Pollock, T. *Managing Creatively.* Boston: Cahners Books, 1971.

Prince, George M. *The Practice of Creativity.* New York: Harper Row (paperback) Collier Books, 1972.

Reed, E. *Developing Creative Talent.* New York: Vantage, 1962.

Rieser, Dolf. *Art and Science.* New York: Van Nostrand Reinhold Co., 1972.

Rowan, Helen. The Creative People: How to Spot Them. *Think* New York: IBM Corp. Nov–Dec., 1962, pp. 7–15.

Samples, Robert. *Introduction to the Metaphoric Mind.* Reading, Mass.: Addison-Wesley Publishing Co., 1976.

Watson, James D. *The Double Helix.* Pasadena, Calif.: Atteneum Press, 1969.

Photo and Illustration Credits Index

1-1, 7-6: By permission of Biblioteca Ambrosiana, Milano. From the Codex Atlanticus, figures 37 and 86 in *Leonardo DaVinci: The Royal Palace at Romarantin.* by Carlo Padretti. Cambridge, Mass.: The Harvard University Press, 1972.

1-2, 1-3: Reproduced from the Catalogue of the Drawings Collection of the Royal Institute of British Architects, volume 9 Edwin Lutyens, published by Gregg International, an imprint of Avebury Publishing Company, England, 1973.

1-4, 6-3, 6-31, 11-1: Reproduced from *Alvar Aalto: Synopsis* edited by Bernhard Hoesli, published by Birkhauser Verlag, Basel, 1970.
1-5, 9-11, 9-19: Courtesy of Thomas N. Larson, FAAR, The Architects Collaborative.

1-6, 2-18, 9-4: From Atkin, William W. *Architectural Presentation Techniques.* New York: Van Nostrand Reinhold Company, 1976.

1-7, 6-32, 11-4: Courtesy of Thomas H. Beeby, Hammond, Beeby, Babka, Architects, Chicago.

1-8: From Erman, Adolph. *Life in Ancient Egypt.* New York: reprinted by Benjamin Blom, Inc., 1969. Distributed by Arno Press Inc.

1-15: From *Cybernetic Serendipity: the Computer and the Arts.* New York: Praeger Publishers, Inc., 1968.

1-23, 7-1, 9-2, 11-5: Courtesy of David T. Stieglitz; Stieglitz Stieglitz Tries, Architects, Buffalo.

1-25: Reprinted from the July 1978 issue of *Progressive Architecture,* copyright 1978, Reinhold Publishing Company.

1-26: Reprinted from the June 1976 issue of *Progressive Architecture,* copyright 1976, Reinhold Publishing Company.

2-19, 9-17: Reprinted with the permission of Process Architects Publishing Company Ltd., Tokyo and Lawrence Halprin. Copyright 1978. From *Process: Architecture No. 4 Lawrence Halprin.*

2-20: Reprinted with the permission of Design Publications, Inc. From the March 1975 issue of Industrial Design Magazine.

3-1: Rendering of the Student Union Housing, University of Alberta at Edmonton, Architects: A. J. Diamond and Barton Myers in association with R. L. Wilkin, Architect. Rendering by A. J. Diamond.

3-16, 3-17: Reprinted from *Helmut Jacoby Architectural Drawings.* New York: Praeger Publishers, Inc., 1965.

3-18, 9-13: Courtesy of Michael F. Gebhart, The Architects Collaborative.

3-19: Reprinted from *Freehand Drawing—Language of Design,* by Michael Czaja. Walnut Creek, CA: Gambol Press, 1975.

3-24: Courtesy of Thomas P. Truax. From a research study, Ohio University School of Architecture and Planning, 1974.

6-5, 7-7, 9-5: Reprinted from *atelier rue de Sevres 35,* by Guillermo Jullian de la Fuente and Anthony Eardley, a catalogue from an exhibition of project sketches and notes from LeCorbusier to Guillermo Jullian de la Fuente, published by the College of Architecture in collaboration with the University Art Gallery, University of Kentucky, Lexington.

6-6: From Richard Saul Wurman and Eugene Feldman. *The Notebooks and Drawings of Louis I. Kahn.* Cambridge, MA: MIT Press, 1962.

6-7, 9-10, 9-12: Courtesy of Gerald Exline. From Williams, A. Richard. *The Urban Stage* (Study Draft). Champagne-Urbana, II: 1976.

6-11, 6-12: From "The Grammar of Ornament/Ornament as Grammar" by Thomas H. Beeby, published in VIA III, The Journal of the Graduate School of Fine Arts, University of Pennsylvania. Reprinted with the permission of Thomas H. Beeby.

6-25: Reprinted from Norberg-Schulz, C. *Existence, Space & Architecture.* New York: Praeger Publishers, Inc., 1971.

6-29: Courtesy of Thomas P. Truax. From masters thesis project, Ohio University, 1975.

7-13: Courtesy of Mark S. Sowatsky. From Atlantis 2, thesis project, College of Architecture and Planning, Ball State University, Indiana, 1977.

9-1: by courtesy of Architectural Publishers Artemis. Zurich. Published in *Louis I. Kahn.* © 1975.

9-3, 9-9: Courtesy of Edwin F. Harris, Jr., '59. From *The Student Publication of the School of Design* vol. 10, number 2, North Carolina State University, Raleigh, NC.

9-6: From Papadaki, Stamo. *The Work of Oscar Niemeyer.* New York: Van Nostrand Reinhold Company, 1950.

9-7, 9-18: Courtesy of James W. Anderson and Landplus West, Inc., Land Planners/Landscape Architects.

9-8: Reprinted with the permission of Lawrence Halprin. From *The RSVP Cycles: Creative Processes in the Human Environment.* New York: George Braziller Inc. 1969.

9-14: Reprinted with the permission of Process Architects Publishing Company Ltd., Tokyo and Romaldo Giurgola. Copyright 1977. From *Process: Architecture No. 2 Mitchell Giurgola Architects.*

9-15: Drawing by ARCHITECT HUGH STUBBINS, from his book *Architecture: The Design Experience.* New York: John Wiley and Sons, 1976.

12-3, 12-4: Reprinted with the permission of William W. Caudill, FAIA; Caudill Rowlett Scott, from his book *Architecture by Team*. New York: Van Nostrand Reinhold Company, 1971.

13-5, 13-6: Reprinted by permission of Harry A. Eggink from the *East Cambridge Study.* by Michael Justin Dowling, Harry A. Eggink, Bruce Leish and Joan O'Riordan, Urban Design Program, Graduate School of Design, Harvard University, 1976.

13-7, 13-8, 13-9, 13-10, 13-11: Reprinted with the permission of the publishers and Steve Levine from *CONNECTIONS: Ways to Discover and Realize Community Potentials.* by Jim Burns, Copyright © 1979 by Dowden, Hutchinson & Ross, Inc., Publisher, Stroudsburg, PA.

13-12: Reprinted with the permission of Peter Hasselman AIA from the *Atlantic City Study.* American Institute of Architects, Regional/Urban Design Assistance Team.

13-13: Reprinted with the permission of John J. Desmond FAIA from the *Phoenix Study.* American Institute of Architects, Regional/Urban Design Assistance Team.

13-14, 13-15: Reprinted by the permission of W. P. Durkee, Urban Design Associates, Pittsburgh and Roy Mann, Roy Mann Associates, Cambridge, MA. from *Portsmouth Study.* American Institute of Architects, Regional/Urban Design Assistance Team.

13-16: Reprinted with the permission of Charles A. Blessing FAIA from *Phoenix Study.* American Institute of Architects, Regional/Urban Design Assistance Team.

Appendix

The following pages contain brief discussions of ideas
related to the content of this book. The two topics,
Visual Perception and Graphic Language Applied to
Architecture, are not included in the main text because
the discussions are exploratory rather than applicable
to the acquisition of specific skills. Nevertheless, I feel
that the ideas are provocative and deserve a small space
for exposition. The discussion of visual perception
considers the impact of recent medical research on our
understanding of perception. The thoughts on graphic
language draw parallels between language and architectural perception or symbolism.

VISUAL PERCEPTION

Most of us define thinking as "something that takes place inside of our head". According to this definition, information arrives at the brain by way of the senses and is stored there for future use. There is an older belief that intelligence or the quality and quantity of thinking depended on the brain that each of us inherited. Today, we realize that the impact of experience is very important and that each person receives information with a different impact even if exposed to the same situation. This accounts for the differences in what and how fast we learn. A *perceptual screen,* constructed from our past experience, is able to select incoming sensory information by rejecting some and allowing some to pass on to the brain. According to some medical studies, this is still a too simple model. These researchers' model (which they admit, still crude) suggests multiple perceptual screens through which the information is processed. Similar to a giant switchboard, these screens are connected to numerous centers of the brain including the sensory controls. This model presents two important points:

1. a very high degree of complex interaction between the processes of thinking and those of perception;
2. when using one of the senses, vision, the perceptual screens developed by the other senses have a definite influence on what we experience.

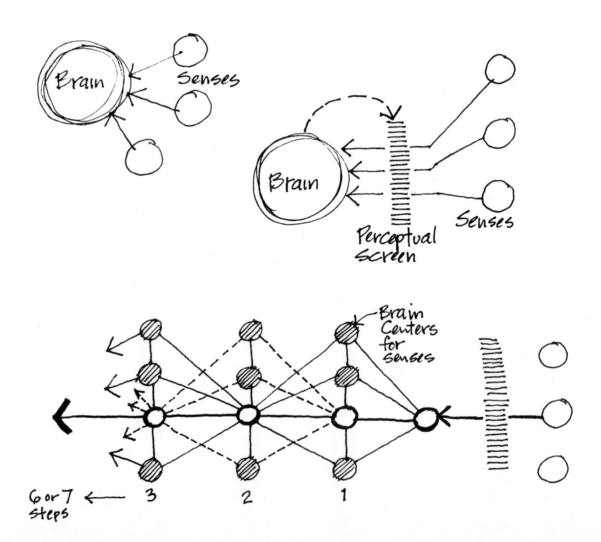

206

The upmost advantage of visual thinking is that while we are hearing, smelling, or touching, we are also seeing; and the brain, which constantly seeks to simplify information for us, sets up visual clues along with other clues, enabling us to substitute vision for our other senses.

The most important function of the brain is to sort or identify quickly our experiences using the most efficient sensory mechanism. Consider this example: look at a picture of a large, sculptural water fountain in the middle of a park. The reflections of the water as it spills and sprays over the edge of the fountain is our visual picture but at the same time, we experience the damp, coolness and the patter of the falling drops. Even if this fountain is only a small part of the total picture, our eyes are invariably drawn toward it because it is visually symbolic of all the other sensual pleasures. Therefore, visual images are powerful by the way they represent experiences using the other senses.

GRAPHIC LANGUAGE APPLIED TO ARCHITECTURE

One of the joys derived from architectural training is the audacity to cross "sacred" artificial barriers in an attempt to see reality. Architecture is not just a built-up environment, it is an act of communication between people and environment. Pursuing the thought further, "man as communicator" cannot be separated from "man as thinker", therefore architecture is really an interaction of mind, behavior, and environment. Living in a house comfortably depends not only on the design of the house but also on our way of life and the perceptions and expectations we have resulting from past experiences. Therefore, the architectural designer must address himself to the client's building, his behavior and perceptions.

Graphic language applied to architecture must represent these physical, behavioral and perceptual realities. Fortunately help is available. In his book, *Existence, Space and Architecture,* Christian Norberg-Schulz pointed out the fundamental relationship between environment, behavior and perception: "Man's interest in space has existential roots. It stems from a need to grasp vital relations in his environment, to bring meaning and order into a world of events and actions. Basically, man orients to 'objects', that is, he adapts physiologically and technologically to physical things, he interacts with other people, and he grasps the

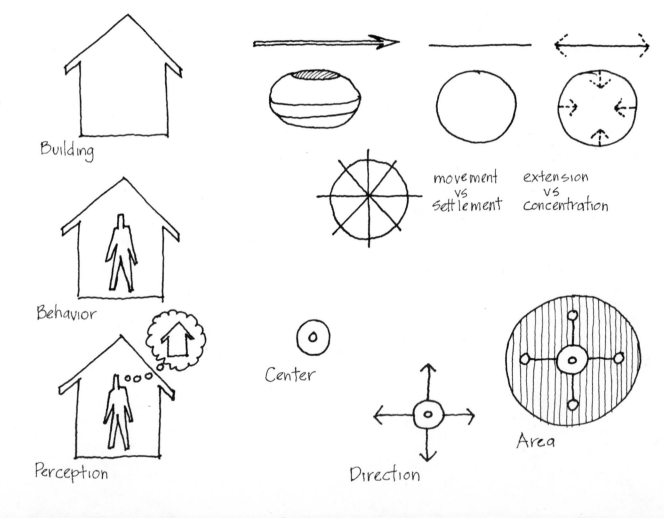

Building

Behavior

Perception

movement
vs
settlement

extension
vs
concentration

Center

Direction

Area

208

Urban Core

City

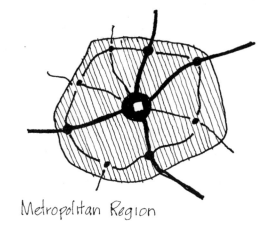

Metropolitan Region

abstract realities, or 'meanings', which are transmitted through the various languages created for the purpose of communication. His orientation to different objects may be cognitive as well as affective, but in either case it aims at the establishment of a dynamic equilibrium between him and his environment." And therefore, our thinking and perception as well as our behavior is conditioned by the environment both cultural and immediate. They share the same symbolic base. If we can understand man's basic interaction with environment, we can identify the basic symbols for that interaction.

Lewis Mumford, in *The City in History,* built his analysis on the concept that "Human life swings between two poles: movement and settlement". These two poles are graphically symbolized respectively by the straight line and the circle. Just as an explanation of our interaction with environment can be built upon the polarities of movement and settlement, I believe that the graphic language for representing environment, behavior, and our perception of environment can be built upon these same basic symbols, the line and circle.

Norberg-Schulz has pointed toward a graphic language for the broad concept of architecture by bridging the gap between perception and physical form. He identified a continuing set of perceptions or an image of the environment as constituting 'existential space'. This 'existential space' is made up of three elements:

1. Center—place of origin or goal,
2. Direction—extension, relationship to context,
3. Area—the limits within which we are aware of centers and directions.

If we refer back to the elements of a graphic language, parallels are clear between Center and Identity, Direction and Relationship, Area and graphic diagram. The elements of existential space are the perceptual structures we use to cope with the environment; they are paralleled by the elements of architectural space—place, path, and domain. The scale of the domain (geography, landscape, urban, community, house, or room) determines which places and paths will be considered.

The same graphic language can be used for both existential and architectural space. "On the basis of a

theory of 'existential space', I therefore develop the idea that architectural space may be understood as a concretization of environmental images, which form a necessary part of man's general orientation or 'being in the world'." (Norberg-Schulz) It is my premise that a common graphic language can be used for all the steps of transformation of abstract, mental images to concrete architectural designs.

Index